T0209296

ASCENDING THE FOURTEENER OF RECOVERY

A Mother and Daughter's Climb toward Eating Disorder Freedom

KC Tillman and Bryn Tillman

ASCENDING THE FOURTEENER OF RECOVERY
A MOTHER AND DAUGHTER'S CLIMB TOWARD
EATING DISORDER FREEDOM

iUniverse books may be ordered through booksellers or by contacting:

iUniverse
1663 Liberty Drive
Bloomington, IN 47403
www.iuniverse.com
844-349-9409

Because of the dynamic nature of the Internet, any web addresses or links contained in this book may have changed since publication and may no longer be valid. The views expressed in this work are solely those of the author and do not necessarily reflect the views of the publisher, and the publisher hereby disclaims any responsibility for them.

Any people depicted in stock imagery provided by Getty Images are models, and such images are being used for illustrative purposes only.
Certain stock imagery © Getty Images.

ISBN: 978-1-6632-4273-0 (sc)
ISBN: 978-1-6632-4297-6 (hc)
ISBN: 978-1-6632-4298-3 (e)

Library of Congress Control Number: 2022913681

Print information available on the last page.

iUniverse rev. date: 10/20/2022

This book is dedicated with love to every woman, man, adolescent or child afflicted by disordered eating. Whether you are the patient, care giver, support system or professional, may our story give you strength and courage while providing hope.

DISCLOSURE

Some of the material in this book could be triggering for those with an eating disorder or suicidal ideations. We have included a list of resources such as the suicide hotline and other avenues for finding help at the end of this book. All information provided is for educational purposes only and does not substitute professional medical advice. It's best to consult your healthcare provider if seeking advice, diagnosis or treatment.

We chose to not discuss weight or provide any ideas that could be categorized as "pro-anorexia" by those that may still be quite ill. On the contraire, this book is meant to inspire many to strive for recovery. There are no extensive references to statistics, studies or works as we felt there to be a multitude of other books readily available to fulfill those needs.

We have also either omitted, changed or just abbreviated names so as to protect the privacy of individuals, except for those who have given their explicit permission—such as our therapists'.

INTRODUCTION/
AUTHORS' NOTE

Who are we, you might be wondering? Well let me tell you. But, first, a warning that you might want to brace yourselves since I will shortly introduce a wickedness from where nightmares are born. The important thing to know about my mom and I is that we are very close. I had friends in elementary school that would make fun of us thinking we were best friends, taunting me that we were each other's diaries. Now though, most of my best friends use her as the community mom because she really is one of a kind! She knows just what advice to give, she unconditionally supports her kids, uses her sense of humor when necessary, and—I've gotta say it— she gives the best hugs. We've had a unique bond since I came into this world. She knows it and I know it. So yes, my mom and I are two crossed fingers of the same hand, wound around each other and I'm proud to say she is on this quest to optimal health with me.

I've grown up always setting impossibly high expectations for myself that produced feelings of inadequacy, imperfections, and failure. As far back as I can remember, I had not had a great relationship with food and struggled with body image. It didn't occur to me that I needed to bring it to anyone's attention. I falsely believed that everyone felt a pang of draining guilt when they ate and had battles in their head about whether they should eat a cookie or not. I thought everyone hated what they saw in the mirror and constantly strived to be a better physical being like I did. Little did I know how wrong I was.

There is another key player in this journey who you should be aware of. His name is Ed. Ed grew up alongside me. When we were younger, Ed was like that pesky little kid that sat behind you in class. You know the kind. The one who laughed at you whenever you said something wrong, called you mean names, basically kicked you whenever you were down. At first you tried to ignore him, but as the years went on you'd start to wonder if he's doing this not because he hates you but because he *likes* you. At some point I started to believe that Ed really wanted what was best for me. Ed wasn't being mean; he was encouraging me to be the best version of myself that I possibly could be through tough-love. With that realization, Ed and I quickly became close until Ed became my best friend. My secret best friend that nobody knew about.

After many years of diet attempts, trips to the gym, different sports teams, exercise purges, calorie counting, restaurant avoiding, and severe restriction, the problem became evident. When my health declined and my mom and my eating-disorder-therapist-aunt, who I happened to be visiting, noticed my eating and exercise habits, my mom started searching for an outpatient therapist for me to see. I didn't want to go to the hospital and leave school, so our compromise was outpatient therapy.

I had weekly check-ins with a dietitian who I liked very much, except for the part about her trying to force me to eat. I ended up lying to her most of the time and avoided the weigh-ins as much as possible, opting instead for phone call check-ins to see how I was doing.

As I continued to lie and go downhill on the health scale, my mom grew extremely worried and refused to watch her baby girl die (which I didn't understand at the time since Ed and I believed I wasn't dying).

The clock continued to tick and I knew that I couldn't get better on my own at this point. The final straw that drove me to this realization was when my mom came to me sobbing that she couldn't bury me. I needed more help than once a week outpatient therapy meetings. Mom put me on the waiting list at the Children's hospital but I plunged for the worst very quickly. Her tenacity pushed her to call the hospital each day until I had an evaluation date. I'll let her talk about the happiness and joyful tears that consumed her after she got the call.

Throughout this book about our constant battle against Ed and his need for control, you will most likely laugh, possibly shed a few tears, and gain some insight through our authentic battle against an eating disorder.

This book is filled with all the pieces that contributed to my complicated recovery puzzle. Whether you have an eating disorder, have a loved one battling an eating disorder, or just want to learn a bit more about the ups and downs and thinking patterns of someone with anorexia, I hope you feel you have opened the right book.

We have limited the use of exact calories and weights to avoid triggering those fighting the good fight.

We wish you the utmost love and strength as you or your loved ones choose to love yourself/yourselves first in this dark time.

All my support, Bryn

P.S. When I do reference calories, I will be calling them sources of energy because truly, that's what they are. Many times, I find the word calories has morphed into a word with a negative connotation, a word meaning weight gain, fat, and too much. Logical Bryn knows that without calories, I would die. Ed is not so aware of that.

Also, in case you're wondering who Ed is, he isn't just some creepy asshole that consumed my life. He isn't a "stalker-ish" boyfriend. Ed is a big, dark, ink stain piece of shit who looks a little something like this: scary, loud, controlling, and endlessly abusive. He is the consistent, painful wars in my head. Ed is my eating disorder and Ed has made my life and my mom's life a living hell. Ed is dead now.

On January 2nd, 2000, I gave birth to a perfect baby girl with a round head, button nose, and the pinkest lips. Never in a million years would I have thought that the precious bundle of joy that stole my heart that day would end up in a battle for her life just sixteen short years later. In 2016 and 2017, my Brynnie-pie and I would end up being pitted against the worst demon we've ever encountered: an eating disorder called anorexia nervosa. This turn of events derailed our lives for over a year, but we were determined to win the battle.

We had the chance to get into a fantastic recovery program and with perseverance, hard work, and many tears, we've come a long way. People often ask me if Bryn is *recovered*. The answer to that is more complex than a simple yes or no. For many years, she had to work at recovery every day just like an addict who quits using substances or an alcoholic who no longer drinks. I can confidently say that five years after entering into the program, she's doing extremely well but we both know that we can never fully let our guard down.

We acquired many tools and found strategies along the way that helped us combat all the monsters that veered her towards the dysfunction of starvation. There were classes and many books. There was therapy: talk therapy, group therapy, art therapy, music therapy, yoga therapy… you get the picture. One of the most cathartic tools for both of us in purging the pain was journaling and writing. Pouring that heartache, fear, anger, and frustration onto page after page was instrumental in our healing journey.

It became evident early on that part of our healing would involve sharing our story to help others combat their own demons. When we decided to turn all of this into a book, it was quite intimidating to be putting so much of our vulnerability out into the world. We decided if we could help just one person or one family it would all be worthwhile. It is our hope that by sharing our struggles as well as the triumphs—even the tiny ones, such as, when Bryn finally ate a granola bar without a fuss—that we might provide comfort to others going through a similarly hellacious and difficult chapter in their own lives.

As I set out to reread each and every page during the editing process, I got discouraged by the realization that a lot of my writings seemed repetitive which may have made the context more redundant. Same feelings of desperation, same stupid words (or lack thereof) to describe how distraught I felt on a regular basis. When I was feeling down about this, I remembered when Bryn reminded me of a passage from the book *The Shack* written by William P. Young. In the passage, God/the Universe/the Source of Love explains why (s)he is patient and is more than willing to repeat the same lessons over fifty times. (S)he explains their patience is because it may take the fifty-first time before one can fully grasp it. Then Bryn would say: "so please keep telling me, it may take me hearing it Fifty-one times". Bottom line, repetition is at times necessary. It is essential to our learning and our understanding and to our growth. It was vital for me in order to fully understand and learn from what I was experiencing. Therefore, I left most of the repetitiveness in just in case it helps in your own journey. There are also passages that are essentially on the same topic but from both Bryn's point of view and from mine. Initially, I thought it would be wise to blend both to reduce the duplicity but upon further reflection decided to keep both versions. The hope is that the reader finds it beneficial, or perhaps even amusing, to see two sides of the same coin. Since this is essentially not only our story, but also our art piece, we wanted to keep it authentic; which may not align perfectly with a typical book layout. For example, there are journal entries that could have benefitted from being broken down into paragraphs for easier readability. I deliberately chose to leave them as one unedited, continuous stream of words without breaks, because that was exactly what our lives were at the time. Long, incessant moments of time that weren't broken down into pretty, easily digestible sections.

Another one of the hardest parts while preparing the collection of our writings was trying to determine how to organize all the seemingly random topics we had written about. We figured we'd go with the tougher times first since that made sense in a chronological order. We broke it down to three essential parts: in the throes of the eating disorder, after being released from the treatment center, and lastly, a year and beyond from hospital admittance. Passages may seem out of place, but just like this entire trek, at times, you veer off course. Sometimes the terrain is rockier and more treacherous and other times you get a reprieve with smoother roads. Living at the foot of the Rocky Mountains, like many Coloradans, we've enjoyed the numerous outdoor activities the area has to offer. Colorado is known for having the most peaks exceeding 14,000 feet, which are known locally as fourteeners (or 14ers). There are Fifty-eight glorious peaks in total in the state. It soon became an analogy at how arduous this process of recovery would be. I kept reminding Bryn that through perseverance we would eventually take in the sublime view with a sigh of relief. The vision stuck and ascending the fourteener became our shared secret code phrase. Because we were in the climb of our lives, it only seemed fitting to use it as the title of this book.

The process of getting Bryn back to health was a rollercoaster of a ride. Our family, including Bryn's younger brother, Cameron, experienced a multitude of emotions. This next passage—also a quote from *The Shack*—really got me through when I was worn down from crying all the time: "Don't ever discount the wonder of your tears. They can be healing waters and a stream of joy. Sometimes they are the best words the heart can speak." And, boy, I can tell you, there were *a lot* of healing waters shed over that intense period for both of us.

Each person's battle is unique, therefore, I am by no means claiming this to be a *how-to book* on beating an eating disorder. We're merely sharing our story through recollections, letters, and journal entries. Our intention is simply to give a glimmer of hope to those in the trenches. I feel it vital to share what worked for us and what didn't because the one thing I clung to with dear life through all of it was that little Four-letter word: *hope*.

In essence, this is a story of villains and heroes. By now you've guessed that the most evil villain is Ed. Being able to defeat Ed once and for all couldn't have been done without two particular heroes—Bryn's therapist, Angela and my therapist, Amanda. Let us not forget that it took a huge amount of bravery (a heroic trait in my opinion) to keep working at recovery when the voice in your head keeps berating you. Therefore, the biggest hero of this story is my coauthor and beautiful daughter, Bryn.

Now, I will leave you with this saying I feel to be incredibly accurate when embarking on any kind of treatment that may be long and laborious since it's not a sprint, rather a marathon:

A journey of a thousand miles begins with a single step.
- Confucius

PART ONE

Getting Help

☙ BRYN ❧

The Lonely Dream

I was at a place, a big place with a lot of people. There was a boy, not much older than me, with a gun shooting at people. I'm not quite sure for what reason but nonetheless people were dropping like flies. I was trying to take him down, to find a way to get him to stop shooting. Once I realized that I couldn't stop him, I began running away from the boy. He shot me in the back of my upper thigh and again through the left side of my torso. I put pressure on my wounds (as they do in the movies) until the scene changed and I was at a hospital. There were a lot of people there, but no one would help me. The doctors refused to operate on me and the nurses wouldn't care for my injuries. I had bullets embedded in my bloodstream and no one chose to give me a lifeline or a chance to survive. Bleeding out, my injuries throbbing with pain, I began screaming for assistance, yet everyone seemed to ignore my existence. Then, a few other people waiting in the waiting room took one quick glance at my lacerations, looked me in the eye, and told me that they weren't that bad and I needed to get over myself. They said, while I was blubbering—and worrying that my life was going to end in this less-than-mediocre hospital waiting room— that I was being a baby. I was in the middle of a crowded room, yet so utterly alone.

I woke up feeling abused and lonely. I keep a dream journal since I usually have incredibly funky dreams. This one is so symbolic of what I'm going through. My mom and I discussed it and both came to the conclusion that the whole dream was a metaphor for what having an eating disorder is like.

The man with the gun, or rather, Ed: shooting me, again and again, no matter how hard I try to fight him off. The doctors and people around me: declining to help me when I'm unable to help myself. The wounds:

bigger than anyone can see or expect, festering inside of me. The others: misunderstanding of my trauma and belittling the pain I'm in— jumping to conclusions and keeping their opinions wrapped in stigma. And the emptiness.

An eating disorder feels so isolating from the world. Even smack dab in the middle of thousands of people, anorexia causes great feelings of loneliness and seclusion which is exactly how my dream felt.

Just as every bullet wound and every shooter is different, eating disorders and their victims are very diverse. Each person has different triggers, different Eds, different ways of reacting to therapy, and different stories of recovery. It affects people in distinctive ways which is something to remember if you find yourself comparing bullet wounds or shooters.

There's no need to compare. A bullet wound is a bullet wound and a shooter will shoot.

🕊 K C 🕊

Raw Feelings

The weeks prior to getting Bryn into a program to save her life, I was so distraught that I couldn't even face trying to journal. But like an infected wound desperately needing to be tended to, I had to purge the pain in my soul. I needed to get the fear out somehow. So I did journal (in a sense). In order to step out of my agony, I wrote in the third person. It helped it to feel a little less raw because it wasn't "I hurt" rather, it was "She hurts"…

1/18/17

Her heart was breaking a little more each and every day. She felt so confused as if she were a lost puppy. How did life unravel so suddenly? It wasn't long ago that people kept priding her on being the best mother they'd ever known with such wonderful, well-adjusted children. Then, in a blink of an eye, it felt as if it were all being robbed from her. Had she deluded herself this whole time that products of divorce could actually come out on the other side unscathed? It appeared so.

In a matter of months, her firstborn, her baby girl, her seventeen-year-old daughter, had developed an eating disorder. The deadliest form of mental illness there is. Her youngest baby, her son, a new teenager, was definitely acting his part by arguing about everything. He was talking back, acting quite entitled and self-absorbed. By looking at how out of control her children were, you would never have guessed that she had spent the last six-plus years of single-motherhood, putting her flesh and blood first. Putting them before anything else. She had sacrificed so much for them out of pure love. She had always thought it was the right thing to do.

Now, she was second-guessing that, along with everything else in her life. Where had she gone wrong? What could she have done differently or better? She knew that laying the blame on herself and feeling guilty were fruitless acts. Yet she couldn't seem to muster up any other logical answers. She was the queen of finding the silver lining to any situation, focusing on the positives, and always believing that everything happens for a reason. Yet this time, her blind faith was starting to slip away. She felt the prickle of injustice magnified by the amount of rotten lemons life had already thrown her way. How much stronger did she have to prove herself to be?

I suppose you could sum up how she felt in one word: alone. So overwhelmingly and bone-chillingly alone.

CONTINUATION ON 1/22/17

Only 5 days had gone by yet she felt more alone than ever. She desperately longed for some support. She felt that all this weight on her shoulders was crushing her. Suffocating her. She was in a state of mental anguish and emotional exhaustion. She didn't even know how she was putting one foot in front of the other, let alone functioning.

She deeply wanted to be able to confide in others that her daughter was slowly killing herself but knew that the world could be harsh with crushing judgment. There was very little understanding or empathy when it came to mental illnesses. She knew that people would think to themselves that she had somehow raised her kids wrong. She knew that stone of blame would be cast at her behind closed doors. Caring about what others thought enraged her even more but she felt too worn down to fight that battle as well.

Her neighbors had gone through a lot when their son was diagnosed with leukemia at the tender age of two. She had tried to be supportive and witnessed such kindness from a vast array of people. Hearts tend to break at the injustice of a baby being the target of cancer. An eating disorder is a different story… People's first reaction is: "they just need to get over it and eat". Her ex-husband had even shown that type of thinking. So how could she reach out for help when so many falsely believed that anorexia is nothing more than vanity?

Alone, she remained.

2/3/17

One simple phone call on a Friday following her three-hour-long assessment came and brought unimaginable relief. The countless days of phone calls, tears, and battles had finally proved fruitful. She had gotten her baby girl into Children's

Hospital. In her opinion, it was one of the best, if not the best treatment program for eating disorders in teens.

She let the following words of solace sink in: "Insurance accepted your daughter's six-week treatment; program starts on Monday". The thousand pounds that had been residing on her shoulders for weeks magically rolled off leaving her in a state of practical gaiety.

Yes, she was so happy.

She kept shaking her head at that word. How could she possibly feel happy when things felt so despairingly awful for so long? It was because hope had been restored. There was finally a glimmer of hope way far down towards the end of the tunnel. She felt like she was at last given a life jacket.

Immense relief.

Her precious daughter now had a fighting chance. This mama bear would be able to go to bed that night and release the horrible thought that her baby could die. She smiled weakly and silently thought: "Not today E.D. demon. Your talons aren't dug deeply into her today... We have made the first step in acquiring the weapons needed to beat you!" She knew that the days, weeks, months ahead wouldn't be easy. Once again, that beautiful four-letter word, hope, shone brightly. Yes, hope would keep her going.

She was flooded with sheer relief.

❦ BRYN ❧

Severity

The severity of an eating disorder tends to be overshadowed by the stereotype of it. Ed and I clung on to denial for dear life. He easily forced a belief of health and wellness onto me. Logical Bryn was suppressed so powerfully that she didn't understand why she needed food. Ed's screams and reasoning bounced around my head day and night— he was so convincing, I felt it irrational to even let the thought that I was sick cross my mind.

How could I be sick if I was so happy? How could I be sick if I looked so thin and beautiful? How could I be sick if I was in control? How could I be sick if I could get up every morning and live my life? Besides, I wasn't thin enough to be anorexic. I wasn't skinny enough to have an eating disorder.

Wrong.

Ed told me those things and I was completely convinced. I never understood why my mom was so scared that she was "going to lose her baby girl." I was right there, wasn't I? Or was that only the Bryn ghost that Ed created? Ed chalked it up to Mom completely overreacting. But Ed didn't know how sick I was.

Ed takes the wheel and becomes a leech on your spirit. He denies everything he is doing, morphing himself to look like your very best and truest friend. He hurts the insides of you. Feeding off the denial, Ed infests your whole body—he seeps into your bones and weakens your heart behind your back. Here are some of the symptoms that can arise from Ed's manipulative ways:

- Developing severe heart problems that may be irreversible and cause heart attacks.

- Your blood pressure becomes orthostatic. Meaning that it changes so drastically from lying down, to sitting, to standing, making it more likely to faint. It causes painful lightheadedness when you stand. It can cause bright lights in your vision that prohibit you from moving. This makes standing upright without tipping over very difficult.
- Your body starts eating itself. Once it's out of all nutrients and fat, it needs some source of energy. Your body turns to eating your own muscles.
- Your body temperature becomes low and the cold you feel is agonizing due to the fact your body turned down its inner furnace. It needed to because your body is trying to keep you alive. To keep in heat, your body starts growing thin layers of hair all over your skin.
- Your metabolism slows down in order to hold on to as many nutrients as possible. Your body wants to stay at a weight it considers healthy. By slowing the chemicals that convert nutrients to energy, the body is attempting to maintain that weight rather than going under.
- As a female with anorexia, you lose your period and could potentially damage your entire reproductive system permanently. Sometimes those battling anorexia are unable to have children— because I was on birth control and I was producing what my adolescent medicine doctor called fake menstrual cycles, Ed told me I wasn't anorexic enough.
- You are likely to develop Osteoporosis. Though most people think of this as something that occurs in older people, anorexia causes bones to weaken due to bone production decreasing and bone absorption increasing.[1]
- Young people between the ages of 15 and 24 with anorexia have 10 times the risk of dying compared to their same-aged peers, according to NEDA.[2]

---

[1] https://www.eatingdisorderhope.com/information/anorexia/kill-spirit-body

[2] *Smink, F. E., van Hoeken, D., & Hoek, H. W. (2012). Epidemiology of eating disorders: Incidence, prevalence and mortality rates. Current Psychiatry Reports, 14(4), 406-414.*
Fichter, M. M., & Quadflieg, N. (2016). Mortality in eating disorders – Results of a large prospective clinical longitudinal study. International Journal of Eating Disorders, Epub ahead of print.

I can check off almost every bullet point above, sadly. And because of these resulting ailments, and the terribly high suicide rates of eating disorder victims, Anorexia Nervosa is considered the mental illness with the highest mortality rate.

❧ BRYN ☙

A Different Life

If you were to wake up tomorrow having a better relationship with food, how would your life be different?

I wouldn't feel guilty about eating, or constantly feel disappointed, or disgusted with myself due to how I relate food and eating with weight gain. My thoughts wouldn't primarily be focused on how little to eat, or what foods to avoid, or worrying about people's judgment when I eat. I would feel like it's a normal activity that doesn't require judgment from others or myself.

Working out and running would be something to enjoy instead of a chore to burn calories and keep me slim. I could feel comfortable, confident, thin, and pretty when I wear a bikini, look in a mirror, or see myself in a photo. I wouldn't feel stressed about eating my next meal if I didn't like what I saw in the mirror.

My life wouldn't be controlled by food. Ed wouldn't constantly be screaming, making it difficult to decipher my own thoughts from his. My head wouldn't consistently be filled with noise.

I could go out with my family to celebrate special occasions and not worry about the calories I eat or if I indulge in an extra piece of bread. I wouldn't have to restrict the whole day in order to deserve going out. I wouldn't sit at the table worrying about the next time I can purge by going to the gym. I could go out to eat with my friends and not make the excuse of having already eaten. I could participate instead of just watching them indulge.

I wouldn't be terrified of food. I wouldn't have to avoid my Instagram explorer or Facebook feed from the terror of food videos suddenly popping up. I wouldn't feel the absolute need to count calories or have self-hating guilt when actually feeling hungry.

I wouldn't have to miss six weeks of school, miss my friends, and feel ashamed when I think of people judging me for this. I wouldn't have to do all this painful emotionally grueling work to fight my eating disorder—to fight for my life.

My life would be very different if I didn't have an eating disorder, but I have to believe that this journey chose me rather than wallow in the pondering of "why did this happen to me?"

❦ KC ❦

Outpouring of love and support

Below are emails and messages after telling some of the essential people in our lives about what was going on. I wanted to give examples of how people, especially teachers, responded with encouragement and kindness. This shows that by sharing our vulnerability, we opened the door for others to also provide support.

<u>Bryn and Cam's middle school French teacher</u>

Hi there,

Thank you so much for your email and for trusting me with such delicate information. I can assure you that it will go no further than me, I know how important it is to be discreet about this. My heart is truly breaking for Bryn. I do remember her as being a perfectionist and understand that she probably used the restriction of food as the one thing she could control (I speak from experience). The problems and pressures of today are so powerful and it upsets me at how many kids experience anxiety, depression or feel the need to be perfect.

I am incredibly proud of her for getting help and have heard how amazing the program at Children's is, they have helped a lot of young people back to the path of being well. I know it is not easy for anyone to seek and go through treatment, but I am sure she is strong enough to face the challenge head-on. I know you must be exhausted too, your lives have been turned upside down and it suddenly turns into day by day. Please remember that you need to take care of yourself too, as hard as that may seem right now. My oldest daughter, now a senior, had some major health problems two years ago and we practically lived at Rocky Mountain Hospital for Children downtown. It takes a toll on you mentally and physically.

Your family has always been near and dear to me and I hope you don't mind me expressing my feelings with you. I wish I had some magic words of wisdom to help make things easier. It will be a long road ahead, but you guys are so loving and caring of one another, that I know you will find the light at the end of the tunnel soon. If there is anything at all, anything, that I can do to help you all out, I will do it in a heartbeat. I will most definitely keep an eye on Cam, but of course not being too obvious. You have great kids and they know how much you love them and want what is best for them.

Would it be okay for me to send a card home with Cam sometime to eventually pass along to Bryn? I just want her to know how she has affected my life and how much I admire her for being brave. If you think that is too much, of course, I will understand and respect your wishes. I appreciate that you checked with her before confiding in me.

I have rambled on long enough I suppose, but please know that I am here for you all in the drop of a hat if you need it. I would love to make dinner for you guys one night soon...are you staying the night at the hospital all the time or would a meal help at home?

Hang in there and please take care of yourself.

Much love,
A

~

A,

Your email seriously brought tears to my eyes. Thank you so much. I am definitely the type to hide under a rock and lick my wounds when going through hard times and have a very difficult time reaching out, thus the fact that hardly anyone knows what we are going through. So just the kind messages and warm thoughts truly help. It's tough because I honestly don't know what I need or don't dare ask (yes, there are some things I need to improve on as well).

I was very sorry to learn that you went through some health issues with your girl a couple of years ago but it's also comforting to know that you can fully understand.

Here's a glimpse at our new normal: we get up at 5:30, leave by 6:15 and are at Children's all day. Bryn is fed 3 meals and 3 snacks a day which is brutal to her (in no time at all that eating disorder voice became very loud). Tuesdays and Thursdays are heavy with parent involvement (the days are really full because she also wants me there for all meals which is the reason I took a leave). I've been taught the meal plans and have to make them daily and Bryn absolutely hates the hospital food which is tough because food alone is hard enough without adding yucky and in her words "unhealthy" foods on top of it all- but that is the eating disorder talking. We get back home around 7 pm-ish, shower and usually fall into bed from exhaustion. This is 7 days a week… Cameron has been living at his dad's which is so hard as I've always had him living with me. I still try to juggle his needs as well. For example, yesterday he had a game at Family Sports Center so I dropped Bryn at Children's, went over and watched his game and came back. Tomorrow is his "Golden" birthday so I'm trying my danged-est (not a word but I like it) to make him feel special, we don't want him to feel he's on the "back burner" so to speak.

As far as all this hell goes, Bryn and I have chosen to see the silver lining (as always) and are determined to one day help others going through this. For the last couple of years, I've voiced wanting to somehow help teens in the arena of anti-bullying and suicide prevention but now realize this is part of that calling and purpose. I don't know how or even when it will happen but I have faith that the Universe will lead me.

Regarding taking care of myself, I will share with you that everything in life happens for a reason and the way it's supposed to for our growth. Last year, in March, I resigned from my highly toxic (yet well paying) corporate job partly due to the pleas of my beautiful daughter as we knew that if I continued to take the abuse, I'd end up having a burnout or worse, a nervous breakdown. My health was taking a hit, my fibromyalgia was at its worst so it was time to take the leap of faith. I managed to get unemployment and spent 6 months of self-care first and foremost: centering myself, exercising again, meditating, etc… In that time, I acquired the tools to manage stress better. Had that not happened, I wouldn't have been prepared to handle what is happening now. So, although we couldn't go to France as planned, and finances were and continue to be tight, I am grateful for that time I had to work on myself and grow, I wouldn't trade it for the world.

I appreciate you sharing your fondness for our family and will say that we feel the exact same way! It's funny; Bryn, Cam and I have always gravitated towards the same "favorite" teachers and you've always been one of them! Also, Bryn would absolutely be touched by a card. The encouragement most definitely

*gives her fuel. Don't feel obligated, however, my just telling her of your wonderful
email brought a smile.*

Ok, talk about long-winded, HA!

You have a great week, and again thanks for the love!

~

Cam's Assistant Principal:

E-mail exchange with Cam's assistant principal whom I reached out to
keep an eye on any potential behavior changes:

ON FEB 7, 2017

Hey KC,

*Had a great talk with Cam today!!! Sounds like Bryn's first day went well and
he is SUPER excited he gets to have dinner with her on Friday!*

We talked about hockey and his upcoming freshman year.

Hope you're hanging in there!

Bryn's chemistry teacher:

Hi KC,

*Thank you for the e-mail. Wendy did send her teachers an email two days ago.
You can tell Bryn that her health is way more important than anything and that
she need not worry about me. The part that scared me most was that I have a good
student-teacher relationship with her but I never sensed any health concern. I'm
keeping her and you in my thoughts and I am hopeful to see her when the time is
right. As I am sure she will begin to wonder and stress about school but you can tell
her that on my end we will get it figured out and to just focus on staying healthy.*

J

Bryn's current French teacher who e-mailed her regularly while she was out:

Subject: thinking about you

Dear Bryn,

I am thinking about you and sending you my best wishes for you to get better. I am looking forward to seeing you soon.

Subject: thinking about you

Bryn,

I am hoping that you are doing better with every new day. I know you might not read this message until later but want you to know that everyone misses you (they don't know about your health). The class is not the same without you. :)

We made animals with paper hearts yesterday for Valentine's Day. Cuteness comes in many colors and styles for sure.

Mme xxxxx

Subject: checking in

Bonsoir Bryn,

Our parent teacher conference night is wrapping up and I thought I would say hello before I head home on the snowy roads. I hear that you are doing better everyday and that makes me smile. [Your friend] shared that she had heard from you and I am happy to see how you decided to do so.

After the presentations on African animals, I looked at wwf because everyone had done a tremendous job at highlighting the struggle animals experience and the efforts that are made by people to help them. I decided to symbolically adopt an okapi. This week I received the stuffed okapi, our mascot, and a certificate. I have asked everyone to suggest a name for her. We will see what the outcome is, but in my mind I call her Brynette because she has your strength.

Keep getting well,
Mme xxxxx

❦ BRYN ❦

The Rules

Ed's rules for me consisted of:

- Always making sure to have loose skinny jeans.
- Always being an extra-small size and occasionally small.
- Eating less than everyone you're eating with. Never eat seconds.
- Always getting a to-go box at a restaurant.
- No carbs. No sugar. Don't dare eat junk food.
- Don't overeat, as in stop eating well before you become full.
- Don't drink anything with calories - only water, coffee, and tea (with stevia).
- Must look the thinnest or smallest in photos.
- Thumb and pinky must touch when wrapped around the wrist.
- Thighs must not touch, having a thigh gap is a must.
- Always suck in my stomach while sitting.
- Don't skip going to the gym.

Ed's rules for me are illogical. I have to break his rules and disobey his commands in order to jump out of the eating disorder cycle.

I realize that the rules Ed applied to only me. They didn't apply to anyone else. I didn't think it was ugly if I noticed that someone else's thighs touched when their knees were together. I didn't consider someone fat if their jean size was over a double zero. I didn't mind if my friends or family didn't take home a to-go box because they ate everything on their plates.

I wanted my friends to eat chocolate, if they were craving it. To order the mac n' cheese, if that's what they wanted for dinner. They deserved that happiness. In my mind, my friends were skinny and healthy. They could and should eat whatever they want. Since I wasn't eating, I pushed my friends and family to eat. I accused my mom of not eating enough during her workdays. I told my friends to get ice cream at the grocery store when they wanted it.

I watched my classmates eat donuts and bags of chips during the second period without batting an eye. I would think, "that's what a normal teenager eats and they don't gain weight or look fat". At this thought, Ed would throw up a red flag and scream at me: "if you think for a second you can eat what you want, you are delusional!" He would insist that I was already fat and ugly and those foods were just going to make it worse. He would remind me how big my stomach was (or how big we perceived my stomach to be) and I wouldn't think of the glazed donut again.

I haven't broken all the rules yet, but I want to. I don't want…correction: I won't let Ed control any part of my life because I want my life back. A big bad bully doesn't need to own your life with rigid rules that only apply to you. You can own your life and for me it all starts with eating the donut.

☙ KC ❧

And who will be the surprise guest for dinner

Meals are just plain anxiety provoking for both of us. As I'm preparing, I try not to get anxious wondering what the response will be when Bryn is presented with the food because I know it needs to be done and is non-negotiable. Along the way there have been many different stages. Bryn went through a phase where uncontrollable panic would set in if her foods were touching. For a while, I stopped making "one dish" meals that had everything mixed together. There are many types of foods that will cause such distress that I've eased up on serving them, even though I know she needs the continuous exposure. I sometimes feel like I'm walking on eggshells, unsure as to the reaction I will get. It often feels like I repeatedly get my teeth kicked in at meals. Being the whipping post of someone's anger day in and day out gets to be exhausting. But I must remember that the anger is not Bryn. It's an outward symptom of all the inner turmoil.

Angela, Bryn's therapist, came up with a brilliant idea to help us get through meals a bit better. She explained the whole theory of "demons on the boat"—an acceptance and commitment therapy metaphor on YouTube[3]. The premise of it all is that Bryn is trying to steer her boat towards the shore (which is recovery) but all the eating disorder demons are trying to bully her and intimidate her away from that destination, so she starts to steer off course. Instead of letting them instill fear in her, she needs to realize that they can't harm her physically and just accept

---

[3] An Acceptance and Commitment Therapy metaphor from Russ Harris' book 'The happiness Trap or watch it on YouTube: https://www.youtube.com/watch?v=z-wyaP6xX wE&t=106s

that they are along for the ride. Naming them, identifying them, and in a sense, personifying them will help in the acceptance process. We were able to identify many of her boat passengers: Angry Amy, Anxious Alice, Bloated Betty, Distrustful Dennis, Depressed Daniel, Edward the Excuse maker, Guilty Gordon, Unworthy Ursula, and the list goes on. Let's not forget Ed the Eating Disorder—the top Dog. I have some of my own like Frustrated Fred. We would attempt to make light of it by hosting a radio show at mealtime. It would go something like this: "Now welcoming Bloated Betty to our show who is asking Bryn not to eat because she's too full." Or I might come up with "Berating Bob is somewhat getting on my nerves this evening. Can he tone it down a bit?" This prevents us from taking things personally while communicating in a healthier manner so that meals don't escalate into arguments. To acknowledge that Bryn has all these demons riding along, but to not give them the power to make her veer off the trajectory towards freedom is essential.

As time has gone on, meals have gotten better with fewer belligerent guests showing up at our dinner table. Yet, there's always that little faint question in the back of my head: "Who will be showing up for dinner tonight?" Finding new and creative tools on a regular basis really helps in combating this disorder. By switching it up we are slowly prying Ed's vicious talons from Bryn, reducing his hold on her. Most days I'm confident that one day, he will no longer have any grip on her or power over her whatsoever. That's ultimately the goal we're working towards every single day.

❧ BRYN ❧

My Boat

On my boat, the passenger list goes a little something like this:

- Ed the Eating Disorder
- Perfectionist Penelope
- Guilty Gordon
- Bloated Betty
- Angry Amanda
- Distrustful Dennis
- Edward the Excuse Maker
- Anxious Alice
- Unworthy Ursula
- Depressed Daniel
- Outcast Olivia and her twin, Abnormal Anna

Ed, well, you know how he operates.

Penelope says I must be perfect. She keeps unachievable expectations over my head. If I'm not flawless, I'm a complete failure that is unworthy of love, appreciation, or acceptance. She's the one who says I must be productive during all hours of the day and refuses to let me relax.

Gordon creeps up as many times as he can. He tells me that I've put my family through too much. He thinks they deserve a better daughter or sister than me. When mom brings up that she quit her job, Gordon throws a tantrum that drowns me in guilt. He shows up when I don't spend all of my free time exercising or when I eat all of my food. He says that I must feel guilty when I haven't perfectly pleased Penelope. Gordon is close pals with Ed the Eating Disorder and Perfectionist Penelope but he can travel without a pack and show up in situations that are unrelated to the other passengers.

Bloated Betty visits about six times a day (meaning every time I eat). She shows up because I feel constantly full. She absolutely despises having to continue eating after feeling full halfway through the meal. She hates eating two hours after a big meal or snack. She doesn't understand why her hunger cues are still inaccurate since she rarely gets hungry and gets full very quickly. Sometimes Bloated Betty triggers Amanda who is also pals with Ed. The passengers have become a very tight knit group.

Angry Amanda usually takes over when Ed taunts and bullies her. She lashes out in a tantrum full of screams and stomps. She wants to throw plates of food quite often. Amanda yells at my mom. Her blood boils when she feels things don't go her and Ed's way. She feels the need to be defensive because she believes the world is going against her. She tears up magazines to calm down—which is better than throwing plates.

Distrustful Denis has already made up his mind about trusting the EDU (eating disorder unit) and my mom's meal planning. He says they're overfeeding me and have no idea what they're doing. Denis hails Ed's logic and only sees proportions through Ed's skewed lenses. He constantly questions Mom about what kind of food she is giving me and if the amount is correct.

Edward the Excuse Maker (brought to you by Ed) doesn't understand if my weight is under. He makes excuses for food and exercise on behalf of Ed. If I walk around the mall but only go to two stores, Edward says that it doesn't count as exercise. He can't believe there's any way I could even burn calories from that minimal activity. He says it won't drop my weight if I only miss one single snack since Betty says I'm full. Edward is very good at excusing the truth and masking it with Ed's lies. It's hard for me to catch Edward in the act. He's very good at his job, is very convincing, and does it quite often.

Anxious Alice has panic attacks a lot. She doesn't like going out most of the time. She avoids situations that could cause her to become more anxious than she already is. Alice gets anxiety about being anxious which, if you want to get technical, is known as anticipatory anxiety. Due to her main triggers being sensory, she can't breathe when there are loud noises, crowded areas, bright lights, drastic textures, etc. Alice and I are currently working through exposures, so I don't have anxiety attacks during things I used to love like going to concerts.

Unworthy Ursula has been on the boat for quite a long time. Her and Penelope are extremely close and love working together. Ursula often reminds me that I'm not good enough. I'm not worthy of love, acceptance, support, or positive affirmations. She says that other people have it worse than me. If I don't measure up to Penelope's standards, Unworthy Ursula gets pretty loud.

Depressed Daniel is a fairly recent companion, but we got acquainted quickly. He is in charge of the unmotivated moods and overwhelming feelings of gray. He suppresses all of my interest in the things I used to like. He makes me not want to see my friends or really do anything except sleep a lot. He took away the fun in thinking about the future and replaced it with cheerlessness.

Outcast Olivia and her lovely twin, Abnormal Anna, tell me I'm not a normal seventeen-year-old. They terrorize Daniel, Alice, and Ed for not letting me be who I want to be. They get very upset when I leave parties early or have to stay home for dinner when my friends are going out. They say I'm weird and everyone knows it. They also tell me I look funny and my body isn't normal. Their favorite word is normal.

In one of my later therapy sessions, Angela told me about the Demons on the Boat metaphor. She explained how all of the demons get really loud and scary when you get close to the shore. In order to silence them, the captain of the ship will turn the other direction and end up going the wrong way. Finally, the ship is going the right way and though the demons are loud and vicious, they won't hurt you. You have to learn to become friends with the demons in order to keep heading in the right direction.

She suggested I have conversations with my demons and give them my sympathy. For example, when Bloated Betty is having a hard time, I can say to her, "There you are, Betty. I expected you to show up quicker. I'm sorry you're feeling full and bloated. Those feelings are temporary but I know they are uncomfortable."

This way, I'm acquainting myself with my demons but also offering compassion to the parts of me I find are the hardest to accept. Instead of trying to avoid hard feelings, I'm learning to sit in them and let them be a part of me. It helps me to personify the emotions so I can separate my thoughts and talk to them.

Besides, since we all have our demons, why not call them funky names?

❧ BRYN ❧

The thing I want you to know about anorexia

JOURNAL ENTRY - FEBRUARY 21, 2017:

Don't tell me anorexia is simply not eating. It isn't. Anorexia is being terrified of food. It's having an anxiety attack in the grocery store and not being able to breathe when your friends make you eat. It's drinking ninety-six ounces of water a day to fill your stomach with something. It's having your hands constantly in your sleeves because they're purple and freezing. It's goosebumps so extreme that your skin hurts from the slightest touch. It's feeling so guilty for eating one extra cup of grapes that you make yourself run three extra miles the next day. It's having clumps of hair fall out in the shower. It's using all your effort to walk up a flight of stairs without taking a break halfway or letting anyone else see how winded and void of energy you are. It's avoiding lying on your stomach because of the pain caused by your ribs and hip bones jutting out.

Anorexia is not being able to hold a conversation because you're too preoccupied with worrying about food. Wondering when the next meal you'll be able to skip will arise and how you're going to lie about it. It's not being able to concentrate. It's lying to everyone around you despite how much you love them. It's taking full meals to school just to throw them away so your mom will believe you ate them. It's feeling a scary sense of power when you see your calorie intake is below x-amount and a scary sense of shame when they've reached a touch more. It's constant furious battles in your head. It's looking in the mirror and, though you're substantially underweight, only seeing all the problem areas. It's never being good enough. It's panic at holiday dinners. It's making a thousand excuses. It's slowly killing yourself without even knowing it. It's anorexia and it's real.

What anorexia is not: Anorexia is not a shallow, insecure being whose main desire is to look like photo-shopped models on the cover of Vogue magazine. Let me repeat. Anorexia is not conceited and it is not obsessively caring only about your looks. There's so much more to it than that.

Due to the stigmatization of mental health, I find common judgments very off-kilter from what anorexia truly is. Anorexia is absolutely not a choice. Many people believe the simple notion that anorexics simply made the choice to stop eating and can just start eating when they realize it's unhealthy. This is not the case; this disorder is much more complex than something as simple as a choice.

❦ K C ❧
Journal Entry 2/27/17

Feeling very overwhelmed. I have the need to journal more than once a week but am tugged in so many directions that it's hard to find the time to do all the things I want and need to do.

I wish the Universe would take me by the hand and lead me where I'm supposed to go. Should I be writing my "dusty, abandoned" novel? Should I be looking for a new job now that I realize I will have to quit the job at the animal hospital I had temporarily just taken a few months back. I will have to find a job I can do from home in order to keep an eye on Bryn's food intake. Should I be researching various avenues in which I can build a stream of income while I am with Bryn during her recovery? I know I'm lucky enough to be able to withdraw from my retirement and wish I could just let go of financial stress for the time being. Should I be answering emails? Should I tend to things going on with Cam's school and sports? Should I be writing more about this fucking eating disorder that has engulfed our whole life at the moment? Should I read up on this illness or just indulge and read something to my liking that helps get my mind off stupid Ed? Too many things cluttering my mind. Bombarding myself with more to-do's and should's is probably not being very kind to myself, either.

Today is a day filled with so many different emotions, fueled by sheer exhaustion. Mainly, I'm plain pissed off. We have completed three weeks of this six-week-long program and it doesn't feel like the woohoo-halfway-there-point at all. Honestly, it's like I'm at the bottom of a huge mountain looking up at the insurmountable hike ahead… I hate how defeatist that sounds. However, I learned a long time ago that I'm entitled to my feelings and must embrace them for what they are.

Then, my favorite motto comes into play: 'tomorrow is a new day' and it will likely be filled with renewed hope.

But today…today, I want to throw a hissy fit (as Ed seems to do so often).

I'm feeling overwhelmed by the fact that my whole entire existence right now revolves around food and trying to be Bryn's support. Grocery shopping has now become an anxiety-provoking ordeal—not that I ever enjoyed that task to begin with. Then add on the daily meal planning sheets (that I must turn in by 11 a.m. every morning for the next day) and the meal prepping at home, since we've graduated to having breakfasts and dinners outside of the hospital.

Every mealtime and snack time is not only met with dread by Bryn but by me as well. Each time I must equip myself for the outburst of anger or tears. I ask myself: "Will I be met by Bryn, or will Ed be showing up for dinner with his dominant, ugly demeanor? Maybe it'll be mean ole Penelope—which is what Bryn has named her perfectionism and who is as equally mean as Ed is." It's like I have to go into a boxing ring but my hands are tied behind my back. I'm not allowed to hit back, therefore, I take a horrendous beating. Before my wounds have time to heal from the beating I've just taken, I have to be able to do it all over again at the next meal or snack just a few short hours later.

I know this sounds absolutely awful and if any parents new to eating disorders were to read this, they'd be horrified. It is the harsh, ugly reality. But, luckily, not every day feels as desperate as the picture I'm portraying at this second. Is it hard? Yes. Brutal, at times? Absolutely. But all the times that I'm able to remain calm, empathetic, yet firm, I am beating Ed at his own game. Those moments feel victorious.

I've been guided by something stronger than myself, I believe it's the Universe helping me to find creative ways of supporting Bryn through this. I somehow come up with excellent analogies that really resonate with her. For example, the other day at breakfast, she was struggling especially hard with the fact that the food proportions keep getting bigger—this is one of my big struggles right now too, but more on that later. I know I've explained a thousand times before that because she was at a weight deficit with her health being depleted, we needed to get her back up to a healthy weight, yadda yadda. So I found a new approach. I asked her what a plant looked like after not being watered for weeks. I walked her through how the dirt would be all dried out and cracked, the leaves limp, etc... Then I asked what would happen if we watered the plant. I explained that the water would get sucked up in two seconds flat, the more water you'd add, the more it'd just get sucked right up. I proceeded to explain that her body was sucking up all the nourishment in no time at all and burning that energy (yes, even though they were keeping her sedentary during the day). Her body kept needing more so we kept needing to increase the amount she eats to compensate.

It's really difficult having to watch your child in distress over food, to begin with. Having to increase their consumption on a regular basis when they believe you are already over feeding them is overwhelming and maddening. That's where I'm at today. I arrived at the hospital already exhausted. Yesterday consisted of our morning trip here (about a 45-minute drive), then I went to one of Cam's playoff hockey games in Boulder, since they won that, they were advancing to the championship game later that night. I came back to the hospital, got Bryn and returned to Boulder for the game. Bryn had extreme anxiety from all the noise—something that had never happened before. We then had an hour-long trek back home. Once home, I fixed us dinner, we ate, bathed and crashed. Bryn had fallen asleep so I decided not to wake her up for her bedtime snack. She woke me up somewhere around 11 p.m. in a panic, demanding that I get up to prepare her snack because she didn't want to have to supplement today but I was too exhausted to move. Today started off with her being angry. I sometimes feel I just can't win… I'm trying to be supportive to both my kids and it is so exhausting, I could cry.

Anyway, as I got to the hospital, I was approached by her dietician about upping the calories yet again. My first reaction was: "just shoot me in the face". I do realize this is the road to recovery, essential to her health, food is medicine and essentially her chemo. I know I have to be strong enough to keep pressing along but it is the hardest thing to have to present even more food to someone who has such a fear and aversion to it. Again, I'm allowing myself to wallow and feel sorry for myself today but will come back tomorrow with a renewed feistiness to kick Ed's disgusting butt!

I want to end this entry on a better note, so I'll share something positive. Bryn has told me on numerous occasions that every time she completes a meal having fought the urge to throw her food away, she feels she deserves something akin to a sobriety chip. So, the other night, I made a bunch of what I like to call "bravery tokens". They were a complete hit! She truly adored them and they've become such a nice motivational reward. I don't think with how tired and brain-fried I am, I could've come up with the idea and inspiration without some divine intervention. So thank you, Universe! I am beyond grateful.

❦ BRYN ❧

No Gray Allowed

"I'm sorry, we only offer the colors black and white. No gray is available."

This is how my brain works, thinking only in extremes. Ed and Penelope find this extremely beneficial in beating logical Bryn to an exhaustive pulp during fights.

I find it very difficult to understand balance because I have a black-and-white way of thinking. When someone tells me that it's okay to have one cookie every day but not the whole package of Oreos, it doesn't make sense. My mind, when I'm not overthinking, works simplistically. To me, foods are only healthy or unhealthy and there isn't some magical middle ground where you can eat one sweet a day and have that be considered acceptable.

Of course, my black-and-white thinking comes with conditions. I only find myself using this type of thinking in terms of myself so when I see my mom eat a bit of chocolate each day but not multiple chocolate bars (balancing her cravings and diet), I think that's a healthy way to go about things. I figure if she only eats a bit, she won't feel deprived and have a need to binge after restraining. But, I have much higher standards for myself.

My no-gray-allowed thinking also translates to many things in my life other than just around food. With grades in school, if I get anything below an A, it's an F in my book. Regarding friends, I am either popular or wildly lonely. To Ed and I, I'm either fat or skinny because a healthy and *normal* weight doesn't exist for me. In terms of an eating disorder, this body image distortion is named the Beauty or Beast Distortion— when you think about your appearance in extremes it tends to lead to exaggerated conclusions.[4]

---

[4] *Learn more about body image distortions in The Body Image Workbook by Thomas F. Cash*

⚘ K C ⚘

Disillusioned Perception, The Distorted Lenses

One day, early on in treatment, I was trying to explain to Bryn that the way she sees herself is a far cry from how the rest of the world views her. Now, by this point, you may have noticed I'm pretty big on using analogies and metaphors to visually describe exactly what I'm trying to convey. Most often, I have a pair of sunglasses perched atop my head, in this instance they could be used as a prop. I removed them and proceeded to show them to Bryn. I asked her what she thought would happen if I placed an open flame right up to the lenses. She answered that they would be destroyed. I agreed but took it a bit further explaining the process: that the lenses would begin to bubble and melt with the heat. Then I asked what the lenses would look like after they had cooled. I received a simple answer: "they'd look bad". Again, I agreed. I stated that once you put them back on and tried to see through them, everything would be distorted.

"That, my beautiful daughter is what your lenses are like. They are damaged, rendering you to see yourself in a distorted way." I paused as I watched the realization spread across her face while it sunk in.

"So, can you do me a favor?" I asked. She nodded. "Can you please trust my lenses for now?" Again, she bobbed her head in agreement, albeit with a bit more hesitation as I know this was a big leap of faith that I was asking her to take.

As the weeks passed, it broke my heart to witness all these beautiful girls (and boys) in that very program who wrestled with the same distorted way of seeing themselves. So often, I wanted to just scream: "how can you NOT see what a flawless, magnificent miracle you are?" Ed, or whatever name you choose to give this eating disorder is a truly cruel and deceptive illusion. He won't be content until he kills you. If there's any advice I can give, it's to remind your child that they are wonderful in so many ways and that they were made just the way they were meant to be, as well as to trust you in that until they acquire the tools—or the new lenses—to see it for themselves.

About a month into recovery, Bryn reached out to one of her friends that she had met through acting classes. She told her via text what was going on and the friend's response was beautiful. She explained to Bryn that she could understand that the eating disorder made the way she saw herself completely distorted and compared it to being color blind. A person suffering from colorblindness might see something blue as green or not see the beautiful color shade at all. She told Bryn not to worry, that she still saw Bryn as Bryn: the beautiful, crazy talented and funny girl she came to know and love, not just "an anorexic girl". This is yet another analogy I will keep readily available in my toolbox when I need to remind Bryn that her perception is off-kilter and not how the rest of us see her.

I will say that you will have to remind your loved one for a very long time that the way they see themselves is a false perception. The closer Bryn got to weight restoration, the more she felt that she looked fat or disgusting, when the reality was and still is the complete opposite: she truly is beautiful inside and out! And sadly, still too thin to everyone else's eyes but her own.

❦ BRYN ❦

A Failing Anorexic

Ed gets really jealous of other more *successful* eating disorders. When my mom says to me, "Bryn, we're really fortunate because we caught it early" or "I'm reading a book where the girl struggled for months longer than we have," Ed gets really defensive.

Ed says I failed at being anorexic too. If I couldn't even succeed at being anorexic, I'm the most inadequate of all the inadequate. Logical Bryn realizes that succeeding at anorexia means dying but Ed hates to think that other people did anorexia better than I did.

During Program, Ed would yell at me and compare me to the people who had lower heart rates than me or that were forced to be in-patient. My evaluator at the time, who is now my therapist, told me that she wanted to put me in the hospital as an in-patient because of my low heart rate but thought that my emotional state was good enough to enable my spending nights at home.

Ed would compare my weight to those in the Program and what meals other people were eating. He hated when people had clothes that hung more loosely on their skin because of their weight and if the shape of their bones were more flattering than mine.

"See, you couldn't even be a good enough anorexic. They're sicker than you. You don't look like someone who is sick," Ed would whisper in my ear. My mom takes pride in getting me into the Maudsley's Children's Hospital Program when she did because the reality is, if I had waited any longer, I could have developed osteoporosis. I could have lost my ability to have kids. And frankly, I could have died. But Ed wipes that logic away when he thinks that other people starved themselves better than me.

The reality is, aside from what Ed says, there is no succeeding in anorexia. There is success in recovery, in fighting day and night to own your life and find your identity. There is success in taking from the deepest points during your eating disorder and seeing the lessons they provided, learning what recovery has to offer and allowing it to strengthen you.

Success is the fight out of the dark grave Ed created for you, not who dug the deepest.

❧ K C ❧

Random fragmented recollections

Looking back, there were definite indicators that should have keyed me into what was transpiring a bit more quickly. For example, I love baths but only have a shower in my bathroom so when I want to soak in the tub, I must use the kids' bathroom. I would get really annoyed at the clumps and clumps of hair that would clog the drain—being that I was the one to have to clean it up— or the gobs that resided on the ledge of the tub. I honestly didn't think that much of it because it was around fall/winter time and I tend to shed more during those periods. Bryn has a whole lot more hair than me. She's blessed with a beautiful head of long Shirley Temple curls.

There was also the fact that she was always freezing and I ended up with a higher electric bill because I was tired of her complaining despite her running her space heater in her room constantly. I had also purchased her a heating blanket for her bed. Again, I remember always being cold when I was a teenager or even up until the last couple of years really. I just ran on the colder side. So I figured she took after me. Yet, thinking back, her body's ability to regulate temperature had gotten worse. That makes perfect sense once you know that the cause was starvation leading to a low heart rate that doesn't pump enough blood throughout the body to aid with circulation. It makes me cringe to think of that.

Then, there was that day that she nearly fainted after donating blood at school during a blood drive. I remember telling her at that time that they had a weight minimum and didn't think she met it. She just shrugged it off because she wanted badly to make a difference by donating blood since she was finally old enough to do so. Not only did she nearly pass out but the volunteers at the blood bank wouldn't allow her to donate after what had happened. Even that wasn't a red flag to me because Bryn had always been petite.

Once more, hindsight is 20/20.

❦ BRYN ❧

Letter to my body

Dear Body of Mine,

I'm sorry for how cruel I've been to you so often. Calling you fat and nitpicking the smallest, most insignificant blemishes on you was no way to treat you, after all you've done for me. I've never respected your purpose or found the beauty in you that all others saw. I want to fix that.

My dear body of mine, without you I could never have gotten so good at running. I could never walk around the art museum or feel someone hug me. Without you, I could never see a beautiful sunset or hear someone's heartbeat. Without your strength, I couldn't understand chemistry or be able to dance and sing. I could never brighten someone's day with a smile or even smell a cup of coffee without you. I could never see this beautiful world without you or write about my adventures. I couldn't ward off the cold without your goosebumps or live at a high altitude without your adaptability. I know you'll help me when I decide to have kids. I'm so truly sorry that I forgot that without your exquisiteness, I couldn't be me.

You've gotten me so many compliments. I know that without you, my spirit would not have a home to serve its purpose on Earth. I am working hard to nourish you now. I want to lift you up and appreciate you rather than bring you down as I have for many years.

My apologies and future loving, Bryn

This was therapy homework assigned to me. I always loved doing my therapy homework. I know it's helped —and continues to help me work on the building of who I am. It is a tool in creating a new identity for myself outside of Ed. Penelope, the perfectionist, also likes it because therapy homework is considered productive to her.

This letter I wrote to my body recounted the wrongdoings I had committed, the changes I wished to make in the future, and the appreciation I had for all its abilities. Writing it also provided me with a different perspective apart from the eating disorder mindset.

This alternative perspective assisted me in understanding that my body is an incredible miracle. My lungs know how to breathe unconsciously. My heart never stops beating. Each beat flows rich oxygen throughout my entire body so I can remain alive. My skin can heal itself with crusty scabs if I'm wounded, ensuring that I don't bleed out. My eyes light up when I smile or am surrounded by the purest joy. My brain is of preposterous complexity—so much so that according to the textbook, *Myer's Psychology for AP* written by David G. Myers, it processes eleven million bits of information per second but focuses selectively on what information is truly essential.

One of the hardest things for me to find gratitude in has been my hunger and fullness cues. Our bodies are so incredibly intelligent by nature that our stomachs grumble when they need nutrients and tell our brains to stop eating when we've fulfilled that need.

It's a fascinating thought to think of all these organs, muscle groups, neural pathways, unconscious activities, neurons, signals, cells, etc. working together to keep my being alive.

That is what my letter helped me to focus on. So if you haven't ever taken the time to acknowledge the miracle that is your body, may I suggest writing your body a letter? A letter that is perhaps from a different version of you that is divorced from Ed—from a version of you that is searching for freedom and independence. You may be surprised at what epiphanies are revealed to you.

KC

Journal entry
March 14, 2017

This Godforsaken disorder sure is an onion. So many flipping layers that make you cry… Bryn's panic attacks and anxiety are getting worse. We're now realizing that anxiety has actually been there all along but that she was able to control it, first through Penelope, then through Ed, this stupid eating disorder. Since we're squashing Ed right now, all the anxiety is surfacing and bubbling over.

Sunday night, Bryn was angry about her bedtime snack and I was so worn out that I didn't have the patience I should have had. I said some things that were mean and hurtful and it turned into an hour-long cry fest with Bryn hyperventilating. I actually called the nurse's station at the hospital because it freaked me out that I didn't have that magic wand to bring her heightened emotions down. She was anxious about school and so many other things and I really should have handled it better but I am human and so very tired of being Ed's whipping post. I set my boundaries stronger than I should have. I know, I wrote something about the "shoulda, coulda, woulda"s and how useless they are. I can't beat myself up, rather I just need to move forward with a focus of doing better next time. Making matters worse, a repeat last night at dinner. I explained sternly that I was at my limits with her anger. It led to tears and another uncontrollable sobbing session. She gets ultra-sensitive when thinking I'm mad at her. It's really like dealing with two different people. She even says how she hates the two people fighting inside of her. All I could do was hug her tight and tell her to hang on to me for dear life until it passed. This breaks my heart beyond anything anyone could imagine. The emotional exhaustion is omnipresent. I've made her sleep with me for the last two nights because I'm so worried about her. I got zero sleep on Sunday night. Last night was much better but I'm still just so drained. Bryn really isn't seeing an end in sight, she feels like she doesn't have a future because Ed is so powerful right now. It's disheartening because I see such a bright future for her. I can't really say that I totally see the light at the end of the tunnel at this very moment either but… I have to claw my way out of this ditch because I feel I have to be strong enough for both of us right now. I've spent days on end trying to find her a therapist, it has been yet another difficult and frustrating process. I have found a couple of options and we actually meet with someone on Friday, I sure hope it's someone Bryn clicks with because trying to find someone who specializes in eating disorders that takes our insurance and that has openings is like pulling teeth.

❧ BRYN ❧

Journal entry -
March 22, 2017

I feel like a HUGE burden to everyone I love and so unbelievably guilty for putting my family through this because they didn't choose me. They didn't choose this. Last night was, up to this point, the worst night of my life. I can't do it anymore. I cried so hard my hands and feet tingled because my lungs physically could not fill up with air. My head and neck ached and felt so heavy on me. I lost it. I clawed at my legs and banged my head over and over on the sink because I needed to somehow let out how I was feeling. It was a whole new level of unbearable.

❧ B R Y N ☙
Journal Entry - March 30, 2017

I'm so done I can't even take it. Part of me just wants to die and be done. I hate my family. Everything my dad has ever done or ever said. Who my brother is turning into. How much my mom makes me feel like shit for everything I do. I get I'm not good enough and never will be. I don't need to be reminded of how I'm not working hard enough or putting enough effort into my relationships. I honestly have no idea why I have friends and I'm sure I'll never have a guy that likes me. I'm fucking nuts and I'm not worth saving so why try?

YOU ARE A FAILURE AND YOUR FAMILY KNOWS THAT TOO. You can't even go back to school. Everyone is going to think you're weak and a failure because you couldn't even get back into school. You suck. And you're not pretty.

Some of the words on the page of my journal are blurred from being splattered with tears. I had never felt that way before Prozac. After I got off the Prozac I was like that too, though. After March 21, 2017, we stopped the Prozac but I didn't improve much. Journal entries up until mid-May when I started on the antidepressant Zoloft are laced with desires to disappear or be gone. I got on Zoloft and became a different person. It was like I was an Aloe plant and someone had just poured gallons of colorfully vibrant water all over me. The gray cloud was gone. I smiled and laughed without forcing myself to press my lips into something resembling happiness. All of a sudden I wanted to go outside and hang out with my friends. I wanted to go on adventures and live, truly live. I became a different person. One with drive and joy. One that saw light and believed in a better tomorrow.

Depression is a scary thing that takes the wind out of your sails and the breath out of your lungs. It's okay to need a little extra help, though it feels risky to be vulnerable. Whether the help comes from medication, support groups, therapy, or a combination of those things, it does not make someone weak or less than. Everyone needs a boost here and there. It's brave and admirable to reach out. It's worth the risk to find some little sliver of happiness.[5]

---

[5] Crisis and Suicide Hotlines listed in Resources

❧ K C ❧

Journal entry April 4, 2017

Well, the more things change, the more they stay the same... Not sure of the validity of that statement but it just came to mind. Things are tough but there is progress (sometimes barely noticeable but it's there, nonetheless) and that *is all I need to focus on. Our therapy session on Friday was rough. We both cried a lot and both felt like no matter what we did (towards the other), it just wasn't good enough. Bryn communicated well that it's not helpful when I tell her that she needs to do such and such so that down the road things are more normalized. I say it to motivate her but she feels it just puts too much pressure on her so I'm trying to lay off those statements. It can get overbearingly frustrating when I feel that we're nowhere close to where we need to be. I know, patience has always been something I've had to work extremely hard at. It's tough when you don't see an end in sight. I wish I hadn't been so foolish in thinking that she'd go through the program and be almost cured. This is going to be such a long road. I must remain in the present. One day at a time. I, at times, miss having a life. Going to meet up with friends, being more carefree but now my entire life is planned around being home to feed Bryn. I do realize that this isn't a forever thing and that's what keeps me going but I still grieve my (temporarily) lost freedom. I was pretty angry on Friday and voiced the one thing I know for sure: that we are capable of changing the way we perceive things and our thinking but this isn't resonating with Bryn. I asked Angela if it's because of her brain still developing or the mental illness and was told yes to both. I was also told that she needs a ton of praise and encouragement right now. I had always believed that you instill a sense of pride in your kids by telling them that they should be proud of themselves instead of merely throwing out an "I'm proud of you". Again, good parenting advice when there isn't a huge life challenge such as dick head Ed. I'm trying hard to provide more praise and reassurance for Bryn. To say that all of this is exhausting is an understatement. I feel even more alone now than ever, although some people are aware of the situation, they have NO idea the hell we're both going through on a daily basis. Ugh, I can't stand how negative that sounds, I refuse to sound like a victim. But, I also know that it's not only healthy to get it out but vital, that's where journaling helps me to somewhat keep my sanity. Therefore, I keep my optimism alive and well and already relish the day that we will look back at this with a victorious smile on our faces. We have another appointment at Children's so I need to go get ready.*

☙ BRYN ❧

One minute recovery

Never good enough. Never trying hard enough. Never good enough. Never trying hard enough. Never good enough. "Try harder. Try harder. Try harder. Try harder. What do you want? What do you want? What do you want? What do you want?" I want to starve myself. "I want you to be better. I want you to be OK." But it'd be easier on everyone if I was gone.

Dear Bryn, I love you. Dear Bryn, I love you. Dear Bryn, I love you. Dear Bryn, I love you. Dear Bryn, I love you. Dear Bryn, I love you. Dear Bryn, I love you. Dear Bryn, I love you.

When you're recovering, one minute can mean the difference between smiles and rainbows and complete meltdowns involving throwing food and slamming doors. I'm not exaggerating. The day these journal entries were written, tears were streaming down my face while my shaky hand was attempting to turn my buzzing thoughts into words. I did not believe what I wrote only four hours after a two-and-a-half-hour meltdown but I wanted to. I wanted to be my friend so I forced myself to keep writing that I love myself.

There are numerous occasions where I will be in a fine mood one minute and suddenly crack the next. I'll be okay and then one word might just send me into a spiral of tears and screams. My mom often says we just need to get through one minute, or even second, at a time. And I have to say, it takes some pressure off when you only have to worry about right now. This minute. Learning to take things super slow on difficult days is worth the effort.

❧ K C ❧

Journal entry: Despair

Drowning in sorrow today. A deep emotional anchored rock is residing within me, sinking me, twisting my guts, rendering me breathless. I am desperately yearning to claw my way out of this hole and scream out for release from the agony that is suffocating me. A beast is trying to take over my baby girl but it seems that a demon of pain is haunting my being as well.

In times like these, I'm too exhausted to see the silver lining, to keep fighting to hold on tightly to that ever eluding sense of hope. Nothing specifically has happened to trigger this desperation; yet it is there, unbudging. Unmovable. Relentless. Tenacious.

I long for peace. And joy. For well being but mostly for my hope to return. I feel lost without it. And scared. The loneliness is becoming overbearing. I would kill to have someone take on my burdens just for a day, an hour even. To have a reprieve from this battle against anorexia and trying to save my beloved daughter's life.

Strength seems to be dissipating. I've made it my specialty to get back up after being pounded by life. Time and time again, I've succeeded in getting back up, dusting myself off and continuing on. This very second, I don't feel strong enough. I'm tired. I'm beaten to the core. I only have myself to rely on, but how can I when there's not even an ounce of durability left within me?

Most times, I'm able to remind myself to ride the wave and that tomorrow is a new day, however, right now, I want to escape this feeling of despair. It's all-consuming and ugly and uncomfortable. I despise negative energy. Yet it is singling me out and bullying me. I feel myself yelling for help from the inside. Not a soul is around to hear those lost, silent pleas. I am so very alone in this and that loneliness is completely asphyxiating me.

Reading back over some of these most desperate entries can prove to be difficult at times. I have often wondered if parents facing their child's drug addiction (a different kind of demon) would use the same words to describe the solitude felt.

When rereading these entries years later, the rock-anchored-in-the-stomach feeling is replaced by the sweet taste of victory. Those times that Bryn thought she couldn't continue, or that I thought I wasn't strong enough were proven to be mere delusions.

❧ BRYN ❧

Loving Food

Often, my mom says to me, "But Bryn you used to love this food. Do you remember when you and your friends loved when I made that for you?" and occasionally the, "even Grandma says you loved that meal."

It's difficult for me to swallow (no pun intended) those statements about my old self loving food because that outside appearance of me loving food was laced with so much internalized guilt. Let me tell you, guilt is not love. Food was tied directly to feelings of unworthiness, inadequacy, failure, being fat, and feeling unlovable. Ed made me feel guilty and like a fat pig whenever the topic was brought up because not only is it mostly untrue, but Ed tells me that it's disgusting if I love food.

It now makes me cringe when I see commercials or coupons that read "guilt-free desserts" or "guilt-free snacks" or "guilt-free" whatever food item it may be because when guilt is inseparable from food, it makes the living necessity of eating much more difficult and less desired than it should be.

My mom often tells me if food were not supposed to taste good, we wouldn't have taste buds; there wouldn't be master chefs that devote their lives to creating the most delicious delicacies. She says that we would eat what dogs and cats eat—the same thing each day just to satisfy our human need for nutrition.

I still have a very hard time telling my mom that the dinners she cooks taste good or if a certain food smells good. I haven't been able to bring myself to the point of saying I like a certain food so I may say instead, "I prefer this snack over the other." I find myself being very hypocritical toward myself because I don't find it repulsive if my classmates, friends, or family express their love of food, only when I do, is it that loving food disgusts me.

❧ K C ❧

Being OK with where you are in recovery

As humans, we tend to want to rush things and can be quite impatient, it is so natural. God knows I'm guilty of this more than I'd like to admit. Oftentimes I question whether or not I'm doing a good enough job in helping Bryn face her fear of food. With the Maudsley approach, you cook whatever you'd make for the whole family regardless of how the one with the eating disorder feels about it. If they refuse to eat it, they can drink a supplement such as Boost or Ensure. This seems heartless but the reasoning behind it is to not accommodate the eating disorder. I tend to make Bryn more safe foods because I feel that this is brutally hard for her with the compounded anxiety and fear. Am I doing her justice? Am I dragging this process out? I'm not sure as each individual is just that: their own person, unique and where they are on their path.

Today, I gave her a heads up that I was about to start making French Toast. Horrible idea. It freaked her out, gave her anxiety and she proceeded to tell me that now, every morning she'd be worried about that prospect. I shouldn't have said anything. Yep, I'm still learning… I told her we'd bring it up in her next therapy session but that we needed to move forward with more variety and especially with exposure to fear foods. Should I just be ripping the bandaid off in one swift, quick motion instead of dilly-dallying around trying to gently pry it off? Probably, according to the family based treatment (FBT) approach. But, my gut tells me I need to let Bryn take the lead sometimes. I'm not saying let Ed take control and I do know that it is at times difficult to differentiate between the two. Shortly after that conversation, we had lunch. She had forewarned me that it was going to be difficult because of that anxiety provoking talk we had just had but she did fabulously well. She even mentioned how proud she was of herself that she was "eating around her plate" more than ever before. Meaning that for months now, she'd start and finish each food group one at a time—instead of a bite of this then a bite of that. That in itself, is huge progress. This realization made me pause to take in the gratitude that although sometimes it feels like we're going at a snail's pace, we ARE moving forward. I need to be ok with where we are at. Progress is progress. Period.

How others take it

I think about the people who surround me with love. I think about how they take what I'm going through. It's a painful thought because I can feel their emotions and sympathize with their reactions to my situation. When I am with my boyfriend or best friends or my mom and am struggling with a certain meal, extremely loud and vicious Ed thoughts, or having a panic attack, I know how hard it must be for them. If I were in their position, free of an eating disorder yet around someone struggling with an ED, I know it would pose its own set of challenges. For me, being a people pleaser with a need to help others in a time of lack, I'd feel rather helpless because unfortunately, you can't force-feed someone you love. There are meals where I genuinely cannot put the fork to my mouth and chew. I am physically unable to move in order to eat. It's like there's an invisible but magnificently strong force field between me and my plate that won't allow me to touch my food. It's frustrating because the mental block is so powerful that I feel at that moment that I would do anything else rather than eat. I can imagine how difficult that must be for those lacking an eating disorder in themselves but experiencing that with me. If I didn't have an eating disorder yet I was with someone who I loved and had a desperate need for them to eat, I would constantly be shouting in my mind, "PLEASE JUST EAT!!! BRING THE FOOD TO YOUR MOUTH, CHEW, AND SWALLOW. IT ISN'T THIS COMPLICATED!!!!" I wonder if my loved ones feel that way sometimes. I'm sure it's human for that string of exasperated words to loop in their thoughts. If it's frustrating for me, I'm sure it's frustrating in a different way for them—they have the added feeling of inability to help someone they love with all their heart. They have a fear of their loved one dying because their voice is not loud enough to combat Ed.

Good, Bad, Foods

My dietitian deserves a gold star for the patience she has had with Ed and I trying to work through the truths of nutrition. I told her that I needed to know why I needed to eat, which led to her spending many of our sessions discussing not only the deterioration that takes place when our bodies are not fed but also how each food group works in your body and why you need it. She gave me a paper that split the food groups into percentages of how your diet should be made up.

I found it very helpful to know exactly how food was used up in my body and why I needed to eat some of my fear foods that Ed labeled as bad such as pasta and peanut butter and cheese. Ed has a much harder time arguing with scientific facts rather than a blanket statement like "all food is good food."

I have heard over and over from professionals with a history of working with eating disorders, from those who have recovered from eating disorders, from books, from my mom, etc. that there are no good or bad foods to a recovering anorexic, your body needs every type of food.

This has been tremendously hard to grasp since I've had such an aversion to unhealthy foods as far back as I can remember and as time has gone on, I eventually developed an aversion to healthy foods, as well. With that said, when my dietitian explained to me that having a chocolate chip cookie every day is not necessarily unhealthy, I'm sure you can imagine how far my jaw dropped towards the ground. After I closed the O-shape that my lips had formed, she went on to explain that each aspect of the cookie—the butter, eggs, the flour, the milk—all had a nutritional need to fill in our bodies. The butter, as a fat, is needed to coat neural pathways in a protective layer allowing firings to happen quickly and efficiently in the neurons. The eggs, considered a protein, are needed for building muscle, and so on.

We talked about intuitive eating and she made it clear to me that balance was the key to eating but that if you only ate chocolate chip cookies, your body would need a variety of nutrients that the cookie alone could not provide. Thus began the work on balance. I was suddenly feeling like a gymnast learning to stay perched atop the balance beam.

The Little Bryn

I think about 6-year-old Bryn quite often. This is the Little Bryn that is hurting inside of me when I don't attend to my body's needs and whimpers when Ed tells me I am a fat, ugly failure.

Little Bryn breaks when Ed pushes me too hard (instead of listening to my own healthy limitations) and little Bryn sobs when she feels she has disappointed herself, Ed, or any of the other 7.3 billion people roaming this Earth.

Little Bryn is the hurting little girl buried deep into the darkest depths of my heart. She feels an incessant need to prove herself to Ed and has an insatiable craving for acceptance—she has a lack of compassion toward herself and a lack of confidence that she occupies with Ed's rare care.

Ed is extremely merciless most of the time and tears me down in more ways than one, creating a need for self-acceptance since technically speaking, Ed is in me and I am in Ed.

This makes Ed's compliments and praises so much more special due to the rarity of them. I feel as if I'm placed on a pedestal of superiority and success when I please Ed. So you can see if I disappoint Ed, what that does to Little Bryn.

While I was very malnourished, I felt intense and irresistible exercise urges. I don't want to go into detail about the compulsive exercises I did so as to not provide ideas or trigger others. But I will say that despite my muscles' weakness and body's nutritional deficiency I worked my muscles and pushed myself unhealthily and to excess.

One day my mom asked me one of those moms-are-usually-right questions that opened my eyes to the neglect I threw at Little Bryn. She said, "If 6-year-old Bryn was very sick, would you make her do squats and push-ups, hurting her fragile little muscles?"

There's that whole new perspective thing again. I realized that I would never hurt Little Bryn the way I was hurting seventeen-year-old Bryn. After that, I hung up a bunch of photos of myself from the time I was two to the time I was six years of age on the mirrors in the bathroom and my room.

Each time I look at them I see the shimmer of happiness in my laughs and cheekbones. Each time I look at them I know I would never starve Little Bryn and deprive her of the approval and necessities she deserves, so why should I muzzle my rights to happiness and nourishment now? If I wouldn't ever dare to abrogate food from Little Bryn, then why would I starve my seventeen-year-old self?

Take that, Ed. Little Bryn will be getting all her needed affection and devotion from me, not you. We don't need you anymore.

Bryn age 6 at Kindergarten graduation

Bryn age 5 at her first dance recital

Support Team

Having a support team is essential in recovery due to the fact that it feels like such a lonely road. At the beginning of recovery, I decided not to be on my phone at all. It wasn't allowed in program but even in the car or at home, I kept it off. I didn't have the energy to reply to friends' snapchats or texts but in the meantime, they could text my mom to see how I was doing.

My mom, at my request, texted a very brief and non-detailed explanation of where I was to a guy friend that I was somewhat seeing—that we will call F1— because I felt that I couldn't keep him waiting for 6 weeks without having any idea where I was. After my first week of Program, I texted him from my mom's phone asking him to come over so I could disclose my situation.

This was going to be the very first person I told besides my best guy friend, F2, whom I will get to shortly. After F1 came over and I explained what had been going on along with a bit about the severity of anorexia, I asked him if he could please let me know his thoughts after he had time to process what I had told him so I wasn't left wondering.

After a week and a half of radio silence, I texted him to ask what was going on. He then went on to break up with me, over text, while I was in the hospital. So the disclosure and non-acceptance of F1, didn't turn out as I had hoped for or expected.

Now, onto F2. My very best friend—who had moved to Montana five months prior to my telling him of my situation—came home to visit in late December. We were both ecstatic to see each other and catch up on our lives (though we mostly knew everything since we talked on the phone and texted constantly). I didn't know how to explain my eating situation to him since this was before entering Program and I was myself, still trying to figure out all the whirl-a-bouts in my head.

He was extremely supportive of me and tried to understand what I was going through. He asked questions and called me every time I needed my person, my pal. He would send me paragraphs of things he loved about me. The day of my evaluation to be admitted into the program he told me that I had to call him afterward to let him know what was going to transpire. He said even if he was at work, he would take the call and excuse himself for a family emergency so that's what I did. We decided my brother and mom would keep him updated until I figured it was a good idea to get my phone back.

The day before my admission he said he was going off the grid and wouldn't be talking to me for a while and wished me luck. This worried me since it was very uncharacteristic of him.

Two weeks into the program and I hadn't heard anything from F2, my mom hadn't heard anything from him, and neither had my brother.

Four weeks into the program, when I finally had my phone back, I decided to text my supposed best friend to share how he'd hurt me when I needed him the most. I illustrated what the length of my days felt like, especially compounded by the betrayal I felt washing over me after an entire month of my person/my pal never checking up on me. He called me the next day to explain that his new girlfriend was madly jealous of our friendship. He said that he was emotionally connected to her and he should have never been there for me as it was clearly a mistake. I haven't heard from him since the last thing he said in our phone call that day: "I can't be with you through this."

So as you can see, F2 was also a bust. My point with telling those two stories is not to scare you from reaching out for help, it's to show that yes, there will be challenges with finding the people who will lift you up rather than tear you down.

I feel unbelievably blessed with the support team I have. Though those two attempts at telling people that I thought I could trust didn't work out in being a part of my recovery journey, I choose to focus on the others I have in my corner—some of the most incredibly loving and supportive people to ever walk this earth. I'm filled with gratitude to have such fulfilling angels in my life that make my presence feel cherished and who encourage me in an array of ways.

Only my closest friends know my story, not out of shame in trying to hide my eating disorder, but because I have chosen my foundation carefully and followed my instincts to find the loyal and trustworthy ones. Those deserving to know the darkest depths of me.

I know it is difficult for them to understand but they offer me support in ways they know how, making me feel much less alone the majority of the time. My best advice is to find those who are little extensions of your heart, your safety—instead of focusing on those who were clearly not worth taking part in your life.

It's okay to have people who break up with you while you are in the hospital or quit your friendship for a girlfriend! If I was able to wipe my tears away and appreciate who I do have rather than those who started on their own separate paths, I know you have the fight in you to do it too.

I've been learning to turn my bitterness, hurt, and anger, into an appreciation for the lessons those trials taught me. They showed me to recognize exactly what I do not want in a companion and I know these experiences are helping to build me to be an even stronger and more complexly beautiful being.

Just like each struggle is doing for you.

❧ BRYN ❧

Depression versus no depression

Extremely depressed self attempting to explain who she is in her journal for the first time since leaving the Eating Disorder Unit at Children's Hospital -May 3, 2017

Well as I said before, I'm Bryn. I'm not exactly sure what that means right now or who I am but I suppose that's just where I am in my recovery- mostly only able to define myself through my eating disorder, anxiety, overbearing perfectionism, and now we're wondering about possible depression. I'll get back to the point where I know who I am, I'm sure of it. I like to think that I am not my eating disorder and I'm certain Bryn is in there somewhere.

I was born in Florida. We live in Colorado, now, in a suburb outside of Denver, called Highlands Ranch. It's a really great place to grow up! I was seven years old when we moved and now I'm seventeen, a junior in high school.

Little parts of Bryn shine through at moments so I'll tell you about that first. Well, for starters, I really love reading. I used to watch TV in my spare time because I do on-camera acting. I'd call TV watching "studying" because I would take little mental notes on the delivery of lines and body language. Now, however, I rarely turn on the TV because I'm going through practically 3 books a week which has been satisfying in its own way. Since the perfectionist in me, we call her Penelope, is very hard on me, my mom & therapist make me read for pleasure mostly because all Penelope wants me to do is read eating disorder books or educational books. Penelope says that if I don't, I'm not being productive which in turn makes me very anxious and triggers a lot of feelings of failure. So, usually, I have the one educational book that I'm reading along with the one pleasure book that I'm reading at the same time. The whole "striking a balance thing" which I find to be quite difficult. For pleasure, I really enjoy the whole dystopia genre but I've also been reading a lot of fiction books with the plot being something along the lines of the main character getting into some sort of accident and then developing a mental illness. I just read this book called Reclaimed and it was fantastic! By the end, you find out that the two twin boys who are the main characters are actually just one person with a dissociative personality disorder. I also really enjoyed The Shack because of the eloquent writing. Another, Crank by Ellen Hopkins, was so unique because she wrote the entire book in the form of a poem based on her teenage daughter's drug addiction. It was definitely dark but extremely artistic. So my reading interests are somewhat all over the place but it's nice to have the variety especially because I want to publish a book one day.

All of these things are the driving force that leads me to write. I love it. I've always enjoyed writing papers for school or just free writing poetry and journaling. I completely agree that writing is quite cathartic and beneficial. My mom and I are pretty close so we want to eventually write a book on our journey through recovery someday because how I figure it, this happened to me for a reason. I've always wanted to take part in something bigger than myself so how perfect would it be if I could contribute in helping others that are battling the same struggle I am?

I'm also a social butterfly. I love being around my friends and spending time with them whether going to the movies or just talking for hours about the enormity of space. The excitement I have for meeting new people is one of my ever so Bryn-like quirks. Making new friends and learning about new people and their interests and their fears and their talents is so intriguing to me. I've always been one to feed off of the energy of other people and jump at the opportunity to be surrounded by my amigos. I find this different because I'm an anxious extravert. Kind of paradoxical. I'm extremely grateful to have such angelic friends in my life that make my presence feel cherished because I know at this age, it's hard to find your people. Only my closest friends know what's been going on with me, and though it's so hard to understand, they try to relate and offer me support in ways they know— like giving me lots of hugs, spending quality time with me, and reaching out because they know I have a hard time doing that right now (plus they always listen to my boy problems and don't make me feel annoying about it). I would never want them to understand what I'm going through to the full extent because they deserve the whole wide world and it would kill me to see them struggling with an eating disorder. But with that said, they're understanding if I don't feel like going out or if I'd rather them come to my house or if I don't feel up for talking and just want to color or even if I'm feeling overwhelmed, scared, or sad, they can relate to those raw emotions even if they can't relate to why I'm feeling them. Right now, I've been pretty opposed to being around others and going to places with a lot of people or commotion. I have to push myself to see my friends, text people back, and do activities with them which isn't like my normal self.

I used to be really interested in photography, loved concerts, found peace in drawing, and craved adventure. I want to get back to being in a happier spirit so I can enjoy those things again. Some additional Bryn trivia: I listen to a lot of music and my favorite kind is alternative. Currently, I am very much obsessed with Bon Iver and Jaymes Young. My favorite scent is the grinds of hazelnut coffee, which to me smell like home. I'm a big fan of 80's movies. I love running. My favorite places are high up where I can see expanses of land (even though I'm scared of heights and of falling). My biggest fear is food. I hoard birthday cards and sticky notes with cute messages on them that have been given to me and put them in what I call my Love Trunk. I am infatuated with the stars. I have a thing for singers named James. I typically have a candle burning in my room. I have a lot of plants and my kitten loves to bat at them. My girls and I have a Sunday ritual of seeing a $5 movie each week. I feel emotions very deeply.

Eating Disorder Story: All my life, for as far back as I can remember, I've never felt good enough. I had issues with what my body looked like and hated wearing a bra. The first eating disorder thought that I can remember having about food was when I was twelve— I ate a lot of Panda Express and contemplated for a few hours going to the bathroom and throwing it all up to get it out of me. 7th grade: my health teacher gave us a website where you can enter what you ate and track your calories so I obsessively did that around that time. 7th and 8th grade: I remember my not-so-biological-but-definitely-part-of-the-family brothers making fun of me for being on a "sugar diet" because I wouldn't eat any sweets. 9th grade: Because I was in tighter clothes for my dance recital, my dad told me I should start doing some Insanity—a popular DVD workout, at the time—because my stomach was too big. I cut out all carbs in order to try to lose weight. 10th grade: I started going to the gym again. I felt guilty every time I ate something remotely unhealthy (unhealthy in my mind was bread, anything with sugar, oils, nuts, cheese, chips, and much more—essentially anything I thought of as fattening.) 11th grade: The guilt became absolutely horrendous and I couldn't take it anymore. I felt fat and hated my body more than I ever had up until that point. The doctor said I was at a perfect weight but I wanted to lose it. I looked up how models became so skinny and decided to go vegan because I wanted to feel better. After doing tons of research, I became very big on the animal cruelty aspect of it all as well. I obsessively counted all calories including the calories in my sugar-free chewing gum and vitamins. My boyfriend of a year and I broke up so I started running a lot. Dad kept shattering my self-esteem in ways more than just my body and food—he poked my abs and told me they were just okay even though I was at the gym 3-5 times a week for about two hours each time while beginning to restrict food intake. Even though I was vegan, I cut out so many more foods that Ed just didn't let me eat. Ed is the name of my eating disorder and Ed had/has a lot of rules for me. It got to the point where the guilt was so bad and so unbearable I just stopped eating completely. I lost a lot of weight really fast and I guess when the hospital weighed me, I lost the percentage of my body weight that determined I was physically anorexic too.

My mom got me into this eating disorder program at The Children's Hospital that's one of the best in the country. It was 6 weeks long from 7 am-7 pm and then once you start getting better you start eating breakfast at home and then dinner at home and then you're out. There, they teach you coping skills and you have a therapist, psychiatrist, dietitian, adolescent medicine doctor, as well as group therapy, family therapy, art therapy, music therapy, yoga, and full family group activities with all the other families in the Program. The dietitians teach parents Parent Supported Nutrition, which is a method in how they feed you. Pretty much, they train the parents for the full 6 weeks exactly how much food in each of the food groups the individual kids need. By the end of the program, we uncovered that I've really had anxiety my whole life but no one ever knew (including myself) because I've always been a severe perfectionist (straight A's, 4.2 GPA, straight handwriting, spending hours on projects and homework assignments making sure they were immaculate) and then the eating disorder covered it up. We tried Prozac for the anxiety and prior to the medication, I'd never been depressed or suicidal in my life, but I got extremely depressed and didn't want to live anymore so I got off the Prozac. I've been off of it for over a month but now we think I've developed depression on my own so I see my psychiatrist today actually.

Once I was out of Program, introducing school back into things and unpausing my life was a shift in gears. School is so anxiety-provoking and extremely triggering to Ed. My guidance counselor is amazing so I dropped two of my classes and only stay at school until 11:30. Still, though, I usually come home and cry or feel absolutely disgusting and blah. Since I've been worse these last few weeks, this week I haven't been going to school because my mom and guidance counselor thought it would be better if we figure out the whole medication ordeal and reevaluate because my stress levels are out of this world. They tell me not to stress but that's like telling a six-month-old to walk— I never have not stressed and I don't know how to not stress. I meet with my therapist weekly, I have weekly anxiety group therapy, my mom and I have tried to go to some energy healers, I've tried homeopathic meds, I debrief with my mom daily when I come home from school so I don't shove my feelings inward. I try to use all the skills that I've learned. I journal a lot, I put time into doing my therapy homework. I also have a mentor that I met through ANAD (National Association of Anorexia Nervosa and Associated Disorders) who I talk to. Despite trying my absolute hardest and giving all that I can give, I break down at a ton of meals and if I'm not bawling, I'm either shaking because I'm so anxious, or screaming because I'm raging pissed at the amount or type of food I have to eat. Typically a hysterical crying episode lasting an hour or two happens about once or twice per day. Motivation used to help me a lot but not so much lately. Frankly, I'm not quite sure how I get out of bed most days. It often feels like I keep getting worse. Since I'm forced to eat and my mom makes my meals, if I don't eat, I have to drink Boost which tastes like shit.

So yeah, not to sound like a totally depressing downer but that's sorta my life. I promise I'm usually a lot brighter and happier, especially when I'm in the not-depressed phase

Slightly less depressed me attempting to explain what has happened, via email to a mentor I'd never met May 14, 2017

It's hard for me to open up about everything but I'm gonna explain what's been going on in my life. I've hardly told anyone because it's really personal and mental illness is very stigmatized but I trust that you wouldn't go and spread this. This is going to be a lot and probably hard to understand, but here goes. I'm anorexic. I started restricting my food intake to a few grapes a day and it got really bad and became an addiction. My health began to become affected. The crazy part is that I didn't believe I was sick whatsoever. I lost a ton of weight and became substantially underweight. I was professionally labeled anorexic. I started losing my hair, I was always cold, my blood pressure was orthostatique—which means when I go from sitting, to standing, to laying down, my blood pressure changes dramatically so I would always get dizzy. The doctors were careful I didn't faint each time I stood up. I also developed bradycardia which means that my heart was too weak and wasn't beating enough beats in one minute (this could have killed me while I slept or given me a heart attack). Despite all of that I couldn't stop because in my head it didn't connect that not eating was harming my body. It still is hard to wrap my head around me needing food to live.

Anorexia damages your body but I didn't feel sick. I know how difficult this is to understand so to make it a bit easier it's just similar to not being able to simply tell a drug addict to stop doing meth. It isn't that clear cut. Similarly, I can't be told to just eat. A drug addict would need to go to rehab to get help for optimal chances of overcoming the addiction, right? Cancer patients need chemo to survive. This is why I was gone for six weeks. I was getting my chemo, it was my rehab, and frankly, without it I would have most likely died. I can at least see that now. I was fed six times a day and had zero choice in the matter. If I didn't eat, I would have to take a supplement drink called boost. They would up it to 150% of my calories for the day. This was like an initiative: eat and you won't have to boost. Restoration of my weight was the priority. I'm still a bit underweight even though we've been doing this since the beginning of February.

My mom quit her job because she is the one that makes my meal plans and has to feed me. Most people don't think this disorder is serious, but its living hell and so much scarier and harder than anyone can imagine. I know it's hard to understand that food is my biggest fear and I get severe panic attacks when I think about food or am in a grocery store or even when someone mentions food but I'm sure you have fears and can relate that way. We call my eating disorder Ed because it's like having a different person inside me that tells me I'm ugly, fat, no one will love me, and Ed says my appearance reflects my character and who I am. If I'm not perfect on the outside, then I'm not on the inside either. Every single time I ate, I would feel tremendous guilt. That guilt quickly became unbearable. The first time I started restricting my diet was when I was eleven years old. I stopped eating sugar before I was even a teenager because I related food to weight gain and didn't want to be a failure.

Long story short, after years and years of feeling this overwhelming guilt and having this voice scream at me if I didn't work out everyday or eat something perfectly healthy, I had to escape the voice. I got to the point where I would only eat 1 cup of grapes and drink 1 glass of almond milk a day. Anorexia's high mortality rate terrified my mom, so she fought to get me into this program. I had a team working with me—therapist, psychiatrist, dietitian, adolescent medicine doctor. It's family involved because that gives the best chance of recovery so there's family therapy and group therapy and art therapy and all this stuff that's helped me on the road to recovery. I still see my psychiatrist, therapist, and dietitian— who have been instrumental in teaching my mom how to meal plan. I'm working at not feeling ashamed of my eating disorder because I am not my eating disorder.

Just like someone with diabetes is not just a diabetic, they're a real person. This is something that I have to overcome right now and am working my ass off to be okay, just taking it one second at a time. We figured out that I have had anxiety for years but coped with it with perfectionism and not eating. I have multiple panic attacks a day where I feel like I'm suffocating and can't breathe and then I bawl and hyperventilate so I'm on medication for that. The eating disorder was something that I could control so I used it as a coping mechanism for my anxiety and to counter never feeling good enough. I'm also an insane perfectionist and if every grade and test score and friendship isn't perfect, I feel I'm a failure. My psychiatrist just diagnosed me with depression also, which is another reason I'm on meds. I know this is probably so confusing, especially since I can't explain it in person. I don't want you to feel like you have to walk on eggshells with me. If you have any questions you can totally ask.

People tend to want to know why this happened. There are many contributing factors: environmental, genetics, societal and boom. Some people develop eating disorders while others don't. One of the biggest causes for me was hating my body and bad self image. I had this incessant obsessive need to lose weight because I've always hated myself. I figured if I was skinny enough, I'd be good enough for once. Maybe I'd like myself. All the professionals have told me that the way I see myself is beyond distorted. Fat and ugly and gross and thinking that no one is going to like me isn't at all what other people see. Ed is a real asshole that bullies me and makes me hate myself. I therefore need to trust others' lenses. I have to trust how other people view me because I can't trust myself at this point in my life. This doesn't mean I'll rely on people for my happiness forever but for right now I have to. I need to believe that if they compliment me or tell me I'm beautiful, it isn't just to make me feel better. That they are genuine. Trusting that others love me for the reasons they say they do while ignoring Ed when he whispers to me otherwise. It's fucking exhausting fighting yourself all the time.

Please don't feel you have to say anything or fix me. I just wanted to be completely honest and share with you what I've been up against since I know you can relate. I don't want to be a burden but if you feel up to responding, that would be great.

The depression kicked my butt. I had never felt feelings like I had in the time I was depressed. It feels like you're on an ice rink without knowing how to skate—each time you get up, you fall on your butt. After a while, trying to stabilize your gravity on those thin blades becomes too tiring so you end up surrendering. You fall, yet again. You remain there, laying alone on the cold ice. You tell yourself that the dark world is too painful and lose all desire to get up and skate.

Because my mom's old therapist's granddaughter struggled with anorexia, she put us in touch. The above letter was my attempt at reaching out. Looking back on it now, it took every ounce of energy to write this due to the fact that this introduction was me attempting to be positive. A contrast to how I felt inside—empty and void of all color. The place I was in was black and rigid. It was a scary place filled with hysterical crying fits that lasted a couple hours approximately twice a day. It was a secluded bubble consisting of only wanting to sleep and never wanting to get out of bed. It was desiring to rip my brain out of my head so that maybe I could get a few minutes of peace and quiet. A few minutes without feeling like there was a giant anchor strapped to my back desperately trying to pull me down to the bottom of an oxygen-less ocean. There were times mom wanted to take me up to the sixth floor at Children's, the psych ward. She didn't know what to do and on many occasions she grabbed her phone to call 911— not because I was trying to take my own life, but because I was psychotically hysterical. Uncontrollable. And she was terrified.

Zoloft saved my life. I know how cheesy and ridiculous that may sound but sometimes the truth is cheesy and ridiculous. I didn't want to have to get on medicine and neither did my mom, not after what happened the first time. Back in program, I was put on Prozac in an attempt to manage my anxiety. Previously to that, I had never been depressed or suicidal. A few weeks into my new medication, I became numbly depressed. I didn't talk to anyone and had completely convinced myself that everyone would feel better if I killed myself. Maybe if I was gone, they wouldn't feel burdened anymore— they would grieve and move on. Carry on with their lives. It was also the first time I ever hurt myself. I desperately wanted the fuzzy fog that was engulfing my brain to clear, the inner pain to cease. My mom found me banging my head against the bathroom sink.

❧ BRYN ❧

An Extension of Fatigue - Journal Entry - May 3, 2017

I'm tired of the gloomy rain drowning my lungs, prohibiting fresh breath rejuvenation. I'm tired of cracking mirrors when I accidentally glance at the reflection. I'm tired of wishing I had the legs of the girl going up on the escalator while I go down. I am tired of the hysterical sobs that drench my overly loose t-shirt and flood my all-too-fragile spirit. I'm tired of the ~~dreams~~ nightmares about oatmeal and chocolate bars and milkshakes and french fries and smoothies and forced admission back into the hospital. I'm tired of pondering why my heart keeps thumping in my chest and if Ed will destroy the unsteady rhythm it sings and occasionally screams. I'm tired of identifying myself as "the abnormal girl with the eating disorder, anxiety, depression, and perfectionism who can't help herself."

I have always had expectations of myself to be the best. This also means that I have to be the best eating disorder patient and the best at recovery. I find it to be quite exhausting trying to be the best all of the time.

I have had days filled with waves of hopelessness and strong urges to give up but I am now learning to accept those days and emotions, through self-compassion. I know that sometimes I have to let myself sit in those uncomfortable feelings before I can use my skills in order to dust myself off and continue up the recovery mountain.

I've always said that you must have the hard times, the conflicts, the moments when life knocks you over, and a range of emotions in order to have an appreciation for the good times, the laughs, the hopeful moments, and the reminders of love. It's much easier said than done to practice the acceptance of defeating emotions. Heck, I'm not great at it! But, what would life be if everything was fine and dandy all of the time?

Give yourself permission to feel the whole array of emotions even if that includes feeling out of control, overcome that gloomy feeling rather than beating yourself up. Feelings are automatic and it is very much appropriate to let them wash over you.

I have always been one to say, "I'm feeling this way but I should feel this, or I shouldn't have that emotion." My therapist calls it "should-ing all over yourself" which is completely counterproductive and self-sabotaging. To should yourself instead of letting yourself be is setting yourself up for feelings of worthlessness and inadequacy. This is due to the fact that the past is unable to be reconciled with, it's the past. Furthermore, emotions are pertinent.

Next time you are feeling, avoid should-ing all over yourself and instead maybe write about how you are feeling, pick up a good book, or take a bath, and welcome the emotions all while being gentle towards yourself.

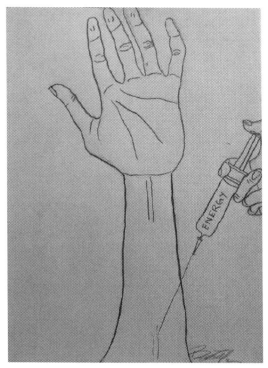

Bryn drawing of extreme fatigue

❧ K C ❧

Ed's blemishing effects on caregiver's psyche

When you set about on this life-changing exploration of surviving disordered eating and striving towards recovery, the challenges you encounter will definitely leave a mark on your very core being. In so many ways, it reminds me of being thrown into the Hunger Games (funny, my autocorrect initially spelled Anger Games—I actually like that). Kill or be killed but in this case, the opponent is evil Ed. In the beginning, your life revolves around the optimum chances of survival: preparing the trajectory to the best of your abilities, then acquiring all the weapons and tools that will give you the best probability of defeating your adversary. This involves all kinds of therapy, staying on track with nutrition and meal plans, reading up and learning as much as you can on eating disorders, communicating more than you ever have, etc… As the months pass, you get glimpses of potential victory here and there in the form of getting out with friends for a few hours, for example, and feeling somewhat "normal" (I despise that word), forgetting for even a split second that your life is consumed with war. Those glimpses are what give you the fuel to keep going.

For months now, I've had very fitful sleep as I have nightmares on a nightly basis. So does Bryn— I've encouraged her to keep a dream journal (amongst all the other journals: a gratitude journal, an affirmations/positive traits journal, and a regular "feelings" journal). These nightmares always have the same theme: I'm fighting something or someone. I am aware that this is my subconscious working out the carnage that this eating disorder is putting my psyche through. It can be draining as some dreams tend to stick around for the duration of the following day due to their vivid and soul trembling nature.

Thinking or overthinking can be depleting as well. I've become a semi-expert at catching adverse thinking and nipping it in the bud. I am human however and when presented with situations that show the uglier side of recovery, I panic at the thought of certain things happening to us. For instance, I gingerly read "Brave Girl Eating" written by a parent of a daughter with anorexia. That book, in my opinion, was the most relatable read yet. I loved it so much that after returning it to the library, I purchased my own copy immediately. So many passages, I felt I could have written myself. However, the ending shook me to my core. Harriet Brown recounts her family's horrific battle with Anorexia with her then fourteen-year-old's diagnosis. She discusses how her daughter, Kitty had a fairly significant relapse at the age of eighteen after leaving home for a brief time. I wanted to cry. They were four whole years into recovery, I couldn't even fathom that happening to Bryn four years from now, my first thought was that there's no way I could ever be strong enough to handle that yet again. I feel I'm barely surviving now, at times. I've clung to the hope that by that point, she'll be sufficiently durable in her rehabilitation to be on her own and nourish her body properly. I shudder at the thought of a huge relapse although I'm very well aware that we are to expect some slips and setbacks. I don't have a crystal ball nor can I anticipate what may or may not happen.

Yesterday, we made our weekly trek to Children's for therapy and ran into one of the mother's of a patient from another state that Bryn had been in program with. We were shocked to the nth degree to hear that she had fallen back into restriction hard again and had attempted to take her own life resulting in her being airlifted back to Children's. This was even more heartbreaking to me as I know that they had been jousting the grips of Ed for six long years already.

Her mother had told me months prior how she had had to sell her house, quit her job, and travel the country in search of the right recovery facility for her daughter who was quickly approaching eighteen, adulthood. Knowing the outcome if she didn't fight to keep her daughter in treatment, she had to get a protective guardianship from the courts. In essence, her life had been put on complete hold, not for months like myself but for endless years. She has not only had to fight the eating disorder but also a copious share of other issues such as debilitating depression and self-harming behaviors. I remember her telling me how she could never leave her daughter alone, and had to hide potentially harmful objects and medications. I felt such gratitude back then that Bryn didn't have to have 24/7 supervision as I don't know if I could have even managed that. When I tried to offer some sort of comfort, yesterday, it was apparent that she was shell-shocked, numb. I attempted to provide support explaining that she appears to be suffering from PTSD like symptoms which would be completely understandable. I know that I often feel that way, even though I haven't been on this journey for as long as she has. Do I have to state the obvious being that it is excruciatingly traumatic having the thought that you could lose your child? That encounter was yet another blemish to my psyche. I could potentially write a whole book on the effects that Ed has on us versus a mere few pages here and there. I by no means intend for this to come across as defeatist, it is however my own view on it at this present moment, my profound yet ugly truth. I will reiterate that I give it my all on a daily basis, to embrace hope regardless of the multitude of horror stories I hear, come across or live through. To all those struggling, I send up silent prayers for strength to kick Ed's ass.

Journal entry May 18, 2017

A somewhat blah day today as it snowed and is cold which is crazy with summer break starting next week! I feel I need to be writing more right now, yet the words seem to have abandoned me. I feel worn out from the constant waves pounding at me. Even though I'm staying in the moment with just focusing on today, I'm left exhausted and lonely.

I found out on Tuesday that Bryn's weight was down! That is the most defeating feeling. It's true that because she's been battling me more over the portion sizes, I tried to back off a bit to see if it'd make a difference. Well, that along with her newly incorporated exercise did make a difference. I'm trying to fight the anxiety I feel surrounding food right now. When I go to the grocery store, I can hardly breathe. When I serve something a bit more challenging, I brace myself. It's like walking on eggshells. I finally told her she needs to stop asking me if I added butter or olive oil or... It makes no difference what's in it. I told her that she doesn't ask the doctor what exactly is compounded in her medication, food is her medicine and she needs to just trust that I know what I'm doing. She keeps challenging me, feeling I don't know what I'm doing. What's difficult is you can't make someone trust you or have faith in you.

Today we see Dr. S, Bryn's psychiatrist. She'll probably up Bryn's Zoloft because she's still somewhat down in the dumps, although we haven't had a hysterical crying fit in approximately ten days—which in itself feels like a miracle. She has shed some tears in that timeframe but it wasn't a full-blown devastating cry-fest. I just want to see this beautiful daughter of mine happy again and free from this demon that is trying to control her. It's not like an abusive boyfriend that we could get a restraining order against because Ed resides WITHIN her. I feel like I'm on my knees begging God or what I call Universe or Source (of love) to exorcize this monster once and for all. Yet, I know only Bryn can do that with a shit ton of hard work, therapy and time… Argh.

I'm going to stop now because, again, I feel that I have no mental capacity to find words accurate enough to describe the despairing emotions. And writing wasn't cathartic today, it brought even more yuck to the surface.

❧ BRYN ☙

Cold Feet

I was watching the Disney movie *Moana* last night with my mom, which is a big guilt challenge in itself. I remembered that the first time I saw that movie, my feet were cold. They weren't just any kind of cold, though. My feet were anorexia cold—the cold you get that feels like frostbite and stems from not eating enough.

I had seen Moana while visiting my extended family, which included my aunt who is an eating disorder therapist, ironically enough. I must admit, my cold feet really tainted the whole experience. Instead of enjoying the all-too-catchy songs and storyline, I was preoccupied with trying to figure out how to position my legs in a way that would help warm my feet. Without any luck and seriously wondering if my toes had turned purple, despite my thick fuzzy socks, I ended up sitting by the fire for an hour and a half once we returned home from the theater.

A few weeks before that, my family and I had gone to see our traditional Christmas movie at the movie theaters. The entire movie, as I watched Will Smith grieve his son's death, I couldn't stop thinking about food and getting home to have a glass of tea to curb the dominating stomach pains which stemmed from having only had a half of a cup of juice that day. I remember having been snippy with my family and not too in-the-holiday-spirit, which wasn't like me. Thanks, Ed, for spoiling the moment.

I have to engrave those tainted memories in my understanding of Ed and his ways. I find that when I'm grieving my eating disorder and hear Ed pleading for me to get back together with him, it would be an effortless decision to run right back into his arms.

He twists all of the bad times we had, turning them into minute and insignificant flashbacks, painlessly tossed aside so I can see only the happiness he provided me. Looking back, I can see that the agony I lived, that Ed very successfully disguised as joy, had seeped into every experience. I know that even if I have to look hard to find that pain caused by Ed, it is paramount in keeping myself going forward on the Recovery Road. Healthier than looking back longingly at Ed in the distance.

Because Ed is the most deceiving, abusive dunce ever, I have to crack the skewed perception of perfection he provided me with and remind myself of the misery framing the life I was living.

I have to remember my cold feet.

❧ KC ❧

How could I not have known?

Now this is a question I'm sure every single parent has asked themselves when faced with the reality that their child's eating disorder is utterly a gigantic monster. I know I have, probably a gazillion times although I try my hardest to squash those unanswerable questions because what purpose does it serve to dwell on them? None. We all know that the "could-as, should-as, would-as," are useless and a waste of time and energy. However, I'm choosing to delve into the subject a bit in order to make you feel that you're not alone in often wondering if there was something, anything you could have noticed sooner or done better. This is not a free pass to beat yourself up, though. Guilt is another energy thief that doesn't do any good. It serves to zap your precious energy needed for the fight of your life and that of your child's.

On several occasions, Bryn and I would have discussions about her feelings regarding Ed, usually on the decently long enough ride to or from the hospital. One day, she was casually talking about how she remembers feeling guilt surrounding food as far back as elementary school and I literally felt like my jaw had gaped wide open. I immediately asked her: "how did I not know this?"

I said: "Bryn, you've always told me everything, how come you never mentioned this?" It came out that she never thought to talk about it as she had assumed that everyday people probably felt guilty after feeling they over-ate or indulged in less healthy foods such as deserts. She reminded me that in the seventh grade, she went on a sugar strike; thinking back, I had just thought it was a fad. Did I kick myself at being stupid and/or blind?

You betcha. But I know all too well that it is in the past, I don't have the option to rewind, I don't get a *re-do* and I can't go back to possibly try to see the seriousness of it. We can only move forward.

When she talks about having had body image issues for quite a while, again, I cringe because I remember thinking back then that all girls hate their bodies to a certain degree. I just never knew how much she hated hers. She kept that from me. As much as she says I have mad intuition, I never did zone in on the severity of her body image problem. Then I start asking myself why SHE developed an eating disorder when nearly all girls complain about their looks. Especially since she had a pretty healthy dose of confidence in other areas. Early on in therapy, she began reading a book called "Life without Ed" that her aunt who is also an eating disorder therapist had sent her and a part of this book described the scenario perfectly: Some girls casually date Ed, some just fool around with him then move on and some commit to him and even go so far as to marry him, which was Bryn's case. I thought that was such an easy way for many to understand part of the complexity of how it targets some and not others (and to varying degrees).

There are times when my negative self-talk states: "you should have seen it coming with her being such a perfectionist". Really? Again, my higher self definitely knows what a bogus statement that is. How many perfectionists do you know that did not end up with an eating disorder?

There have been so many other times that she would shock me with a piece of information that would just make my jaw drop. Recently, we saw a trailer for a movie we had seen all together as a family. This was in the month of December before being admitted to Program. We had had a longstanding tradition—since they were little—of seeing a matinee movie a few days before Christmas in order to slow down a bit from the hustle and bustle of the Holidays. I stated, reminiscing, what a good movie it had been and Bryn spoke of remembering her stomach pains from hunger distracting her from the movie, she admitted she had only had a cup of juice all day that particular day. I was mortified, I had been home, how did I miss that? She continued on to admit that while visiting family in Canada that same Christmas break, they went to a Disney movie and the whole time, her feet were so cold she felt like they were frostbitten. The pain from her cold feet completely took away from that experience. Again, I could beat myself up over and over again with the I-should-have-knowns but we have learned and been practicing self-compassion which entails not "should-ing all over ourselves".

Bottom line: save yourself some trouble and self-abuse by abstaining from posing questions revolving around "how did I not know" and focus on putting all of your energy into helping your loved one beat the destructiveness of Ed.

Part Two

Life After Program

❧ KC ❧

The very long road
to recovery

I was taken aback when I realized that Bryn's six-week treatment was merely the itty bitty tip of this giant iceberg. I'm sure some might think that naive, however, I was so focused on just getting her the help and saving her life before her being admitted into Children's, and then getting through each day during Program. I hadn't fully prepared for the *after* part.

Program is pretty much designed to restore health and weight, give some coping skills, teach the parents how to take parental control back over food and never negotiate with the eating disorder. Once life resumes, therapy continues but oftentimes it didn't feel like enough support to either Bryn or myself. It was plain hard. New disordered eating behaviors that Bryn had never dealt with before would pop up, to our surprise, only to be told that it was quite natural as we were trying to squash Ed. He would keep throwing fits by trying to maintain his position in Bryn's head and life.

I think the hardest part of this *after* phase is not seeing the light at the end of the tunnel. Not having an end date per se. All you can do is focus on the here and now, the present moment, each day, each hour, each minute and work hard on keeping the faith and hanging on tightly to hope. Not an easy task, especially if you tend to be an impatient person as I often feel that I am. You have to constantly remind yourself that setbacks will happen but that you're still making progress. Some days the steps are just a tad smaller. And that, my friend, is okay. This ordeal has definitely helped me to improve my understanding of mindfulness and acceptance, that is for sure.

❦ BRYN ❦

Recovery Kitten

I had wanted a kitten for a while. Mom said no because she was allergic to litter boxes (not really, though, this was just her excuse for hating the smell). When we were in the waiting room to be evaluated at The Children's Hospital determining my association with the Eating Disorder Unit, I thought up the idea of a recovery kitten. My brother had been saying he wanted a dog for his birthday but I told my mom that if he got his dog, I should be able to get my kitty.

Each day at program, we had to fill out our check-in sheet which consisted of our daily and long-term goals as well as our motivators. A lot of days I wrote down *recovery kitty* as a motivator to get through each day.

One of the times mom and I were doing crafts, she found a picture of a white and gray kitten with bright blue eyes so she cut it out for me and I hung it up on my desk. I saw the picture of this kitty and melted, it was perfect. The thing was, though, I wanted to adopt a kitten and not buy one from a breeder but sure enough, the day after I got discharged, my mom's friend, knowing we were looking for a kitten, called us to come to the adoption center. They had just gotten new cats from Louisiana.

Originally, we went in to look at a different kitten but my sweet little Indus caught our eye. She was really little and shockingly, the spitting image of the magazine hanging on my desk. She let me cuddle her which is exactly what I needed for my anxiety. We had already bought all of the kitten essentials: toys, a litter box, food, a cute food bowl, a pooper scooper, the whole deal, so I got to take her home that day (freaking happiest day ever).

Now the reason I'm telling you a story about my cat in our anorexia book is because she helped me. When I was feeling sad or anxious, I held my kitty. But most importantly, I knew that I would never starve my kitten.

I have to feed her just like I have to feed myself too. It was good for me to care for something because it showed me that I need to care for myself and love myself like I would Indus.

When we got her, she was underweight from living in an abandoned house along with the stress of traveling. Once she got settled at our house, she started eating up a storm. I got to see her natural instincts—since she was underweight and her little body was malnourished, she knew, intuitively, that she needed to eat more to get back to health and grow.

She's now more comfortable with us and she meows for her food, she also begs at the table just like our Pomeranian-Chihuahua dog does. She pushes Kodee, our pup, aside to eat his food and Kodee takes the abuse! When I'm eating my nighttime snack, Indus will come up to me, sniff my food, and try to eat it! Last night she ate my graham cracker crumbs and a few licks of apple sauce. I think it is all too ironic that my recovery kitten loves food more than any other cat I've ever seen!

The universe sure does have a sense of humor.

꒰ K C ꒱

The Cat

When Bryn was in treatment, a lot of the kids there were working hard at recovery because their parents had promised them a new therapy pet as a reward. Of course, Bryn jumped on that bandwagon because even before she had gotten sick, she had been begging me for a cat for years. We'd always had dogs but I had given up on cats when Bryn was a baby as we had a cat named Bugaboo who started to pee and spray everywhere in the house after Bryn was born. We had to let him go and that was heartbreaking. Bryn also became allergic to cats in childhood so I would always remind her of that. I'd joke that she's allergic to cats and I'm allergic to litter boxes. Despite holding out all that time, I figured it would, in fact, be a good motivator for her given the circumstances. Knowing full well that she was only a year and a half away from going off to college, I figured it would be a comfort for her until then. It was sure to help with the transition from daily treatment in a hospital setting to working her recovery at home. Before she was admitted, I was working temporarily for an animal hospital inside of a pet store so I would regularly go look at the cats. Therefore, they knew I was somewhat interested and when new cats would come in, they would let me know before even putting them up for adoption. Being that I was still wrestling with the idea and not convinced about getting another pet, I would decline.

A few weeks before her treatment was to end, we were cutting out images from magazines for a vision board when we came across a picture of a cute whitish/gray long haired siamese kitten with blue eyes. Bryn cut it out as a motivational tool, a way to manifest her future cat as I'm a believer in the law of attraction. Literally, the day after she was released, we got a call from the pet store with news that there were a couple of cats that came in and were available including a one-eyed kitten. We had thought *how perfect, a pet with a disability* so we rushed over to see them, intending on bringing the one eyed cat home with us. Out of the corner of my eye, I spotted this beautiful kitten in the corner that looked exactly like the kitty Bryn had cut out from the magazine. We discovered that this five-month-old kitten had been found in an abandoned home in Louisiana and brought to Colorado. After a lot of debating, Bryn came to the conclusion that she indeed did manifest this beautiful white and gray Siamese with blue eyes. She decided to name her Indus after a star constellation (my big dreamer and hopeless romantic- the apple doesn't fall far from the tree). We brought Indus home a couple of hours later.

There are so many ironies that come with this cat that has stolen our hearts: first and foremost, the biggest thing we noticed is her passion and obsession for food —probably due to the fact that she was a malnourished stray and had been starving at the beginning of her life. She's always curious about what type of *people* food we are eating and begs worse than the dog. Pretty perfect for an anorexic, no? Here we are a few years later and we still laugh about it. Also, Indus bonded to me more than to Bryn and that's mainly because I'm home all the time and Bryn, as she has regained her independence, tends to be on the go a lot. I still tease Bryn and tell her on a regular basis: "thanks for getting *me* a cat, Bryn". Or I call Indus my cat which Bryn immediately retorts: "*My* cat, you mean". I would joke that I despised litter boxes and was allergic to them. Well, Bryn truly is. She gets stuffy and sneezes when she has to clean it. The cat is also long-haired and has curly hair, just like Bryn. I've never seen a cat with waves in their fur like that! The final kicker? A few years back while vacationing in Louisiana, I was robbed of my wedding ring. It was an awful violation especially since that ring was to one day go to my son. But now, I figure karma somewhat returned a *gem* to me. Seeing the humor and serendipity of it all, I'm in awe.

Magazine clipping of kitten used for motivation

The actual cat we ended up manifesting, our sweet Indus

❧ BRYN ❧

The Biggest Loser

After all these months of digging inside myself and working through the compilation of experiences and genetic predispositions that developed Ed, I had completely missed my obsession with the TV show, The Biggest Loser. From fifth to eighth grade, it was my favorite show. I would watch it each week with my little brother and dad while eating dinner (and usually ice cream for dessert). Ed cringes at my admission to that.

Looking back, I see all the things that could have helped shape Ed. Bob Harper on multiple episodes would talk about certain foods the contestants needed to stay away from, even after they had been eliminated. No salad dressing. It has the most calories. Don't drink your calories. Never eat sugary sweets. Turkey has less fat than ground beef. Stay away from all foods deemed slightly unhealthy. They would exercise all day, every day— it became their life. If by the end of the week, one of the contestants gained one pound, they were considered failures and were sent home with an arising fear of putting on weight.

Yes, of course, you're probably thinking, "Those contestants are overweight which causes its own set of problems. They're just trying to become healthier." Well let me tell you when you have body dysmorphia and can't see your appearance rationally, you're going to take those weight loss tricks and rules to heart. I've carried them with me all the way up to this point. Especially as someone who thinks completely in blacks and whites, I avoided everything the trainers told the contestants to avoid. Before Program, I don't remember the last time I had salad dressing and if I did order some, it was always on the side. I looked up how to get a personal trainer and became addicted to google searches on weight loss tips. I saw myself as overweight and fat which to me meant, losing weight was the only option. That is what the show portrayed: if you're overweight, you should do something about it. So I did. I wanted the praise they got. I wanted to be seen as successful and beautiful. I wanted to love my body.

After the winner, Rachel Frederickson—who clearly had lost enough weight to practically qualify her as anorexic—made an appearance, there was much controversy. I didn't know how dangerous anorexia was and thought she was doing a good thing for herself but I saw how everyone else reacted. Still, I didn't completely understand why viewers were so worried.

Unfortunately, we live in a society that is obsessed with body image, dieting, and weight loss. Unachievable expectations are placed upon us through photoshop and underweight models. Everywhere one turns, an advertisement about Weight Watchers, FitTea, tummy tucks, Shape-wear clothing, etc., smacks us in the face. Yet at the same time, McDonald's encourages super-sized meals and if you skip dinner, you're labeled as having an eating disorder.

Now, even the name makes me cringe. I don't need to cut out foods and have a daily gym membership to be a champ. I don't need to obsess over my weight and breakdown if I gain a pound in a week. "Are you the next Biggest Loser?" No. I'm the next biggest winner because I eat every meal. I'm the next biggest winner because I kick Ed in the ass day in and day out. I'm the next biggest winner because I am on the road to health.

❦ K C ❧

Family Based Treatment and Cognitive Behavioral Therapy

The Maudsley approach is a family based treatment in the sense that it involves the entire family in solving the eating disorder. It actively engages the parents in the restoration of the child's or adolescent's health. This was the method used at Children's hospital. After being released from that program, we were urged to go to weekly group CBT therapy that focused on exposure therapy. The intent was to learn to develop better coping and thinking patterns to combat the mounting anxiety. The hope was to reduce Bryn's anxiety especially towards food. Unfortunately, the opposite happened. Just having to go was causing extreme anxiety for her. I told Bryn that we needed to fulfill the entire six or eight-week commitment. That it would eventually get easier. It didn't and as much as I have always held my kids' feet to the fire with finishing anything they start, I accepted that, with certain conditions, we could withdraw and find a method that would be more helpful and less anxiety producing.

I found that doing mindfulness work at home such as visualization, meditation, positive affirmations, and breath-work was more helpful and Bryn found greater success in reducing her anxiety. I knew that this was one of the times where you have to pick and choose your battles and I'm glad I wasn't so rigid in making her finish that group therapy because it truly was hindering her progress. I know from many things I've read that cognitive behavioral therapy can produce great outcomes, so please don't be discouraged if it's a route you've chosen. I'm going to go into the repetitive territory of overstating that each individual and each approach is unique. My perspective on individuality is hopeful as it gives many combinations that can potentially help.

❦ BRYN ❦

I've noticed you gained weight

For all my recovering eating disorder fighters out there, I'm sure you can relate when I say that, "I've noticed you've gained weight" is one of the worst things you could hear. But, my best friend said that exact thing to me and I didn't keel over. So, I assure you, people who can't relate to eating disorders or don't know what to say may say something very triggering or hurtful without thinking twice about it. It doesn't mean they don't love you or that you look ugly or fat (like your eating disorder may try to tell you). But you'll just have to continue fighting through the pain and maybe laugh about it after shedding some tears.

At one point in time or another, most recoverers get a comment that makes their eating disorder go wild— whether it's the "you don't look like you have an eating disorder" or "are you trying to lose weight too?" or "oh, I see you've gained weight". Any one of those comments feels just as belittling and jaw-dropping as the others.

When my best friend told me she noticed I'd gained weight on my second day back at school after returning from Program, my heart sank. It took all of my might to not break down right there in the middle of my high school's hallway. I ended up going home after the second period and do you know what I did? I still ate. I ate the snack my mom gave me without throwing the granola bar in a raging fit or feeding it to my dog. Now I can look back and laugh that someone who knew what I was going through could still say that to me but at the moment, all I wanted to do was rush back into Ed's arms and let him comfort me.

I realize now that the reason my friend said that to me was because before I left for the hospital, the way I looked scared her. She thought I looked unhealthily skinny and, though I wore very baggy clothes, my wrists, boney hands, and purple fingertips worried her. As my best friend, when she said that she'd noticed I put on weight, she meant it as a compliment. She knew me gaining weight was what I needed to do in order to be healthy and really meant the comment out of love. She knew, even though I still couldn't wrap my head around it, that gaining weight for me was necessary. And it was not only necessary, but it was beautiful.

❦ K C ❧

Journal entry 6/2/17

Sitting in the ski lodge at A-basin, feeling content that I was able to provide a fun day of snowboarding for Cam, one last time this season. I feel he's had to sacrifice a lot with me not being able to do things for him that would be all-day events since life has consisted of meals/snacks every few hours. I would have liked to ski myself but with not working right now, I couldn't justify splurging on a lift ticket. Plus my ankle injury from last October is still causing me some pain. This is the first time in months that I have left Bryn to do "food" without me. She is lucky to have A and L to help her along. I couldn't have asked for better friends for her. So, they were all going out for breakfast (a big challenge that Angela has been prodding Bryn with) and basically, the girls order whatever they're having for Bryn. When it comes to snacks, the same thing: they portion out whatever they'd eat. I love it, it really is helping to normalize her with what a typical teen would eat. So, we'll see how today goes but I think it's huge progress! Oops, well, there goes that thought. She just texted me, "I want to die. Have never wanted to starve myself more." Yikes. I just don't even know what to say to that… I guess it's to be expected. It's tough because I try to teach her that thoughts and words are powerful. I'm big into the whole positive thinking and manifesting/ law of attraction way of living and share it all with her but I am not sure that she's able to fully grasp it. I know that the prefrontal cortex is still forming in the teenage years, rendering teens to rely more on the amygdala (associated with emotions, impulses, and aggression) for decision making, so maybe it's unrealistic for me to think that she's capable of mind molding herself… I know that even adults find it difficult to recondition their brains but damn it, I'm living proof that it can be done! Oh well, not going to dwell, as Bryn has told me, she needs me to be repetitive for it to all sink in….

☙ BRYN ❧

Afraid to leave the abusive BF

JOURNAL ENTRY - JUNE 9, 2017

I have never wanted to starve myself more. Bathing suit shopping made me want to stab myself in the neck with a fork and rip my hips off of my body. Is that possible? Can I change the shape of my bones yet? Maybe if I wish hard enough I'll be able to. Accepting my body seems more and more distant as the days go on, as I keep eating. I watch my friends eat KFC, pizza, french fries, donuts, Oreos, Goldfish, with their glass of lemonade all in a span of like eight hours. None of them are fat! They're all perfectly healthy with these slim bodies and nice asses. "Can I do that?" Bryn wonders before Ed throws a tantrum causing hurricane force winds of guilt for even letting the thought cross her mind. The answer Ed gives is an astounding "no." Shocking, right? Here's the catch. If I do that, I will be a fat whale, a pig that disgusts everyone around her (and I mean more than I already am). They all already see that I'm overweight so I know they would be wondering why I'm eating anyway. I know Angela would say I could eat fast food more than once a week and stay healthy. My nutritionist would tell me that it's considered normalized eating to do that, especially since we're teenagers. But Ed and I say no. No matter how hard we try to be "normal" and wear a bathing suit to go to the pool, and go out to eat with friends, and watch what they consume, I will not be normal. Because I have Ed so normal doesn't exist for me. I'm caught between this limbo of dying due to starvation and not living due to not starving. Which one is worse?

I didn't expect to love my eating disorder, to want to care for it and let it flourish in me. I didn't expect to want my eating disorder, to make it my best friend and find comfort in it. As a recovering anorexic, I now have to grieve the death of my eating disorder and grieve the life I had with it.

I wasn't prepared to have this feeling of great loss during recovery but it feels as if my best friend has died or I've had to break up with the love of my life who provided me sanity and comfort. Ed gave me a sense of control when I felt lost and he sometimes would give me compliments which were very special since most of the time he's a real dickhead. It made me feel like I had value and a purpose.

I often think about going back to him, even though he's like an abusive husband. He gave me stability and support but at the same time physically and mentally abused me. Somewhere in me, it's nice to know I have the backup option of just returning to the world of anorexia— I find comfort in knowing it's there. Those are Ed thoughts, little pieces of grief still circling around the cycle.

☙ K C ❧

Journal entry 6/10/17

I'm in the middle of having a garage sale but needed to vent so desperately, out of sheer frustration. Bryn has had several bad days in a row and it's frankly wearing on me. I'm so tired of being a slave to this eating disorder. The other night, Bryn had a friend over for dinner before going to youth group and Cam was also here for dinner. It had been a pretty tough day, we had trauma-sensitive yoga but Bryn was feeling so anxious, she got through almost all of it but then had to go outside and wait for me to be done. I had already meal planned for homemade macaroni and cheese (had to think of something that both Cam and her friend would enjoy as well) and knowing it's a big fear food, I only gave her a small portion and supplemented the rest of her plate with veggies and garbanzo beans (which if you go by the Maudsley program, already is wrong, you're supposed to feed them what everyone else is eating, period—no discussion). Well, needless to say, Ed reared his ugly head and had a fit. Bryn refused to eat the mac n cheese so I told her she'd need to supplement with Boost. Another fit as she hates that so I only had her do a shot glass of it then had her supplement the rest with a protein shake that she likes (problem is that one is quite a bit more expensive and I give it to her daily as it is in order to get more calories and nutrients in. Again, I'm acquiescing to the flipping eating disorder when I'm not supposed to be). Although we had "guests" for dinner, I still had to be firm and explain that we need to move forward and progress. Of course, that was interpreted as: "you're not progressing". I mentioned that as it is, we're taking things slowly because her therapist, Angela, already set a goal to eat not one but TWO desserts over two weeks ago, we haven't done that yet as Bryn just isn't ready. I also stated that yes, it'd be easier on me too if I were to always feed her the safe foods (which I pretty much do, again, not the right thing as far as Maudsley goes) and that was also mean. There's that stupid fine line again of pushing (equivalent to ripping the damn bandaid off once for all) or not putting her under stress and letting her take the lead and challenge herself. She fought with me about the fact that I chose the worst day to present a challenge food, that I was cruel to bring up the desert issue, that she challenges herself all the time, etc... It seems I'm up stink creek without a paddle. Last night she baby-sat and chose to go to a friend's beforehand so I asked that I bring her dinner where she was babysitting. I did, although exhausted from the garage sale. Then, when she got home at 11:45, she had to wake me up for her nighttime snack (knowing I'd be up at 6 am) because she still can't eat on her own (especially since Ed has been so loud for days now). Does that sound like I'm a slave to this dang re-feeding process? YEP. But, what alternatives do I have? I'm imprisoned, I either do this or she goes back to starving herself. Great options, huh? Yesterday, Cam was here so he manned the garage sale while I went in to make Bryn's breakfast and eat with her (she cleaned up and had a fit because I left the empty granola bag on the counter and she saw the calories), then I allowed Bryn to make some mega big smoothies for our lunch (that way she could come out and drink it with me: easier when eating outside of her comfort zone which is the kitchen table with the ongoing scrabble game going. However, I'm not sure it was enough caloric intake). Today is a different story, Cam's not here and Bryn woke up already in a foul mood, apparently and said that she refused to eat breakfast in the garage. So I had her compromise and drink a big glass of bottled smoothie drink & eat a banana in the garage (quicker than having to eat a bowl of granola which she refused to do, not a big enough breakfast but it's SOMETHING). But initially it was quite the battle, I told her that ultimately if she refused to eat, that was on her and if her weight was down again on Tuesday, we'd be bumping up the meal plan. I also told her that since nutrition was the number one priority, if she refused to eat, she'd have to cancel her plans. She, of course, called that a threat, I told her it was a consequence and the way I was taught to approach it with the Maudsley program. I also tried to explain that she needed to be flexible and not have such rigid thinking and that this was yet another example as to why I don't think that a road trip to Utah in a month and a half was foreseeable, she's just not proving to be ready for that. Of course, that was yet another threat to her. I simply said that it wasn't after she yelled at me that she's having a bad day (third in a row, by the way, granted it is a full moon too) and I said: "yes, what happens if you struggle this hard on your road trip?" And she told me she'd just deal with it. Yeah, I'm just not too sure.... So, she finally came into the garage, drank the smoothie, ate the banana and shortly after, came out and said she was riding her bike to the library. It's so hot today and she was in jeans, didn't want to take water, refused to put on sunscreen, that's her newest self-destructive behavior and she's already burned several times and

I've explained the consequences being skin cancer which runs in the family, wrinkles, damaged skin, etc... but she doesn't give a crap. She still lays out in the sun without sunscreen daily. Again, what do I do? Let her live with the dire consequences? That's like saying: "ok, don't wear your seatbelt and live with the consequences if you crash and get injured or die". The thing is, I'LL be the one with the consequences of having to take her off life support. I've explained this same thing to Cam about biking and skateboarding without a helmet. They don't listen. So, do I take the bikes and skateboards away, do I refuse to let Bryn lay out in the sun? What the hell am I supposed to do??? And who has the answers for me? Opinions are like buttholes... right? But, I need guidance here. I felt that up until this point, I had been a pretty dang good mother and I'm still bending over backward for these kids, I think I've almost made them over-indulgent. Then, I start to question: have I turned them into spoiled brats? Am I enabling this eating disorder with Bryn knowing that I'll stop at nothing to "help" her? Is this so-called help (of still making her meals, eating with her, etc...) actually a crutch? I've been writing this off and on for an hour now and am not feeling in the least bit better (hard to smile and be friendly as people are coming and going when all I want to do is cry). I am heavy-hearted, frustrated, angry, sad and most of all: lonely. I have no-one to confide in (my last counseling session was all about progress so it seemed that I was doing ok and could probably back off therapy a bit- HA!). I try hard not to even go to the dark places in my mind and stay in the present and accept that we are where we are but I have to say that is so hard sometimes. I just want Bryn cured of this evil illness! I'm also starting to wonder if we need to bump up the Zoloft yet again or include the Abilify (from my understanding it's an antipsychotic that helps with such rigid thinking) but I'm leery of adding more meds. She just needs to do the work. I know she is but right now, it seems that Ed has the upper hand with her and I don't know how to change that besides helping her with thought challenges (which aren't helping at this particular moment). So, because I'm kind of focused on this garage sale, I'm backing off somewhat so that she can fight this on her own to a certain degree without me holding her hand (she's not receptive to my opinions or help right now anyway). I've gotten good at living in the moment, taking each day in stride but this very second I want to scream, run away, have a life away from dickhead Ed and all his bullshit! Find a support group, you might suggest. I've searched and the only one is clear in Denver right at dinner time and rush hour traffic (from like 5:30 pm to 7 pm), so that hasn't been an option. I'm exhausted from being so alone in all this! Ok, rant over, this is pointless. It's the same shit, different day...

☙ K C ☙

The perfect storm is the answer to the "how did this happen?" question

As I have stated before, oftentimes you find yourself wondering how on earth this could have possibly happened to your loved one. I, myself, have been bombarded with those thoughts on numerous occasions. Throughout the journey, we would uncover pieces to the complex puzzle. Imagine a great big onion that you had to peel, layer after layer; burning the hell out of your eyeballs. We discovered that Bryn's eating disorder developed after the brewing of a perfect storm. Every element had to align consummately. What we uncovered towards the end of Program, is that Bryn has always had anxiety—unbeknownst to any of us, even herself. Early on, she used perfectionism to mask it, to feel in control. When that wasn't a powerful enough tool, she began controlling other things such as her diet and what she put in her mouth.

Over the summer between her Sophomore and Junior years, she'd have sleepovers with friends and, like typical teenagers, they'd eat junk food. Bryn would get blah and feel guilty so she decided she wanted to start eating *cleaner*. She started researching whole foods and veganism and was determined to give it a try. The more she researched, the more it also became an ethical stance leading to the refusal of eating any animal byproducts. I figured I'd support her in this as she really was doing it in a smart fashion, making sure she got enough protein and well-balanced meals. I was also an animal lover and vegetarian before my pregnancy with her. Her dad wasn't thrilled about her not eating meat and wasn't afraid to voice it. We consulted a dietician in order to appease him. I was actually proud of her will power, the research she had done and how smart she was being about it. So, I actually encouraged her, wanting to be a supportive mom. With hindsight, did I help in enabling the monster Ed to rear his ugly head into Bryn's life? Possibly. Should I sit here and dwell on that and beat myself up cruelly? No. I don't think that would be a purposeful use of my time.

Bryn had also begun working out more. I was at a point in my life where I also started taking better care of myself and introduced more walks, yoga, and workouts into my routine. I was striving to align mind, body, and spirit in order to combat fibromyalgia pain but was also on a quest for inner peace, happiness and exercise truly made me feel better. I had just taken a huge life-changing leap of faith by quitting my highly toxic corporate job because it was literally killing me. I was working hard at taking care of myself in order to be a better mom, a happier version of myself. So, when I noticed Bryn focusing on exercise, I honestly thought that it was for the mental benefits as well. I figured it to be a healthy way of dealing with stress, especially when so many teens turn to drugs or use other unhealthy coping skills. I was proud of her. I hadn't realized that it was driven by a hatred of her own body and what she saw in the mirror.

Then, a couple of months into her Junior year, she quit her restaurant job as a hostess at a steakhouse due in part by the disgust of seeing meat served but mainly because it was too much with her endeavor towards perfect grades, auditions & acting as well as weekly volunteer work at a hospital. She was getting stressed and run down so we had to pull the plug on something. She used her free time to get workouts in. Shortly after, she and her boyfriend ended things on their one year anniversary, right before homecoming. She was completely heartbroken and angry so she dealt with her rage and sorrow by running and going to the gym. Anyone who has been heartbroken knows that you tend to also lose your appetite somewhat but I figured that too would pass. After a couple of months of this, I confronted her about the running becoming too obsessive. She was fuming and lashed out towards me while flat out denying it. But a couple of days later, she went to her school guidance counselor, Wendy, who has always had Bryn's back and came clean about the food restriction and exercise purging behavior. This was around the time of midterms, right before winter break and Bryn's stress was overbearing; which is what I believe led her to admit to the dysfunctional behaviors around food and exercise. She came home and told me about her confession, at which point her guidance counselor and I talked. We figured at the time that we had caught it early enough and that because she had admitted to it, the problem wasn't as severe as it could have been. Bryn spent Christmas in Canada with her aunt and her paternal grandparents because she was touring the University of British Columbia. I thought of reaching out to her aunt, knowing that she was an eating disorder specialist but intuitively knew she'd quickly figure it out on her own and I didn't want to make Bryn uncomfortable. Her aunt did pick right up on it and had a talk with Bryn. However, once the cat was out of the bag, it's as if that gave Bryn free reign to completely restrict. Each day got worse and I was working a job where my schedule was all over the place so I wasn't always home to watch food intake. I quickly realized how fast her decline was becoming and began frantically searching for help. Those days were filled with endless calls and tears because it seemed that door after door would be locked. Begging in desperation for someone to help as this eating disorder turned into a sports car: going from zero to sixty in two seconds flat. It got to a point where I was calling the Children's eating disorder unit daily. I truly thought I would lose my baby girl and was so relieved when we finally got her into their program.

The bottom line is that each event lined up perfectly for this full-blown eating disorder to bully its destructive way into our lives. A horrible secretly kept body image issue and guilt every time she ate along with anxiety and stress being managed through perfectionism; coupled with a new vegan diet and more exercise that opened the door to restriction; top it off with a big heartbreak and BAM: hello Ed. Do I wish I had known all these events would lead to this so I could maybe change the course? Of course. But this is the hand we were dealt so I have no other choice but to play the hell out of these damn cards.

❧ K C ❧

June 24, 2017, Letter to Bryn after an ED argument

My beautiful daughter, Bryn,

I'm writing this letter because I'm very heavy-hearted about our argument last night. I know that in the heat of the moment it's very hard sometimes to communicate effectively and find that at times, I need to sleep on it. Additionally, the written word is easier for me to express.

I will start with the last thing I told you last night: you know that I love you no matter what, always. It's tough for me when your insecurities come out and question that. It's not that you question my love for you but when you say things like: "you expect me to be perfect" or "you don't think I'm progressing enough", that really hurts me. It's hard when people put false words in your mouth. I know that being human, I've at times sent mixed signals or done the "crazy-making" as you call it; but I feel I've rarely ever said anything to imply that you need to be perfect. I feel that when I say things like "keep trying to reprogram your mind" or "you can choose to see/perceive things in that manner", I'm only trying to help you to lead a happier life. It is by no means implying that if you don't succeed at those things, you're less than perfect. First off, you know that no one is perfect and I do not expect you to be. You've always been perfect just the way you are in my eyes. I truly think that when you say those things, it's because YOU expect yourself to be perfect. I also often feel that you expect me to be perfect and no matter how hard I try because I'm human, I sometimes fall short and feel like there's little forgiveness when I say or do something you don't appreciate.

I've discovered lately that everything regarding parenting teenagers is about navigating very fine lines. Last night, I was quite hurt and angry and frankly beaten down by the fact that you tend to lash out at me. Here's where you might say that I send mixed signals: I've always told you that I am your safe person, that regardless, I will always love you and be here for you. But, I also get to the point where I feel that the constant lashing out and taking things out on me over the last few months has worn me down so I feel I have to set my boundaries as well. You see the fine line? I've shared with you several times that I tend to build resentment when I try my hardest to be the best mom I can be but feel that there's little appreciation and/or feel disrespected. Yet another fine line: when I try to demand some respect but don't want you to take what I'm saying and feel guilty. I share my feelings with you so that we can both learn from things not so that you'll drown in guilt. I very often feel like no matter what, I can't win. I know you feel the same way many times. We might need to work on that together in order to get rid of those ill feelings that the other expects more from us. I really do accept you for who you are, I'm merely trying to help shape you into a strong woman who has inner peace and joy.

My biggest desire is for you to be happy, I want the best for you. When you're hurting, it breaks my heart. When you're struggling and I try to help but it backfires, I feel that I'm inadequate in being able to help you and that's when I try to troubleshoot and bring up the fact that maybe we need more outside help. It has nothing to do with you trying "hard enough" but a lot to do with me feeling I'm not "good enough" to get you through this battle. Those feelings are brought on even more by criticism: me saying the wrong thing or expecting more of you or whatever it might be. On a daily basis, I try to show you that I'm supporting you and cheering you on by the notecards or rewards or the "chips", so when you tell me that I expect you to be even better, it hurts me deeply and I'm left not even knowing how to defend myself on that. And that's when I really question if I'm capable enough of being your foundation of support.

I want us to continue to be a "team" not fight each other like we are enemies. I need us to come up with better strategies for your venting your anger so that I'm not the brunt of it and so that I don't get angry back. I don't ever want to crush your spirit, I want to help build you up. It's hard to do that when I feel attacked and feel the need to defend myself…

I love you with all my heart, Bryn. Let's get through this together!!!!

❧ BRYN ❧

Self-compassion

See, I've never been one to be healthily selfish. I never wanted time for myself nor would I ever turn down an offer from my friends. I didn't focus on myself or give myself a lot of downtime. Since I can remember, as far back as grade school, I was always on the go go go. I had homework to do and teachers to email and textbooks to read and sports to play and extracurriculars to participate in and volunteer work to help with and money to make and friends to hang out with and spaces to clean and games to play and neighbors to see and kids to babysit.

As time went on and I matured, my time to show myself some compassion was focused on my friends. I was there for all of them at the drop of a hat, no matter the time of day. I would be constantly texting and giving advice about boy problems and caring for other people's insecurities— continuously tending to those around me. As an empath, that's exactly how I wanted it. It's how I liked it. It's how I needed it. Because I liked and needed to feel needed.

Fast forward to driving to the hospital with my mom, and we were discussing my own expectations of myself versus how I view the expectations of others. I told her in my exhaustion and frustration, "If one of my friends gets a B on a test or in a class I tell them, 'Wow good job! That's a good grade and you worked the hardest you could in order to get that grade. Don't beat yourself up about it!' But if I get a B, I'm mean to myself and second guess what I did. I tell myself, 'Oh you should have tried harder. Maybe if you studied more, you would have gotten a better grade.' It doesn't matter if I get an A in the class, I need an A on every test, every single one. And if I get 94% instead of 97%, it just isn't good enough."

My mom, taken aback by the pressure I put on myself said, "I want you to be your own friend. Treat yourself the way you would treat your friends with love, acceptance, and support." I think about that conversation a lot because it's easy to be your own worst critic but that only hurts you. Since I struggle so much with the guilt of being a burden, I challenge that feeling by reversing the roles and being my own friend. If I had a friend in my position, with an eating disorder, battling anxiety, depression, Ed, and perfectionism, I would never feel that their coming to me for support was a burden. I would feel honored that they chose me as a part of their support team and I would give them all the help and love I could.

I figure that is how my friends feel about me. If I were my friend, I would give myself a hug and state that I tried my best for an A and the best is all I can give. I would say to myself that being me *is* good enough.

With that said, it's very difficult for me to accept when others (such as my therapist, mom, mental health counselors, friends, etc.) tell me to take a break and do something for me since I've always done for other people. Penelope (my perfectionism) says I must be productive which means reading educational books while standing up, cleaning, or writing my own books. My psychiatrist thought-challenged that with the concept of being productive in relaxation.

With practice, I've gotten better about taking a bubble bath when I want to or coloring instead of reading. I'm not quite good at the whole production-in-relaxation thing yet but I keep trying and on the days I don't finish all of my homework or clean the whole house, I tell myself that it's *okay*. Today, I needed to show myself some love by relaxing. Because rest and relaxation are restorative. This does not mean, never do your dishes and watch Netflix all day, every day, but moderation and self-compassion are essentials.

Sometimes—well quite often, to be honest—I need someone to demand that I do something for me. Whether it is my therapist telling me to paint or my mom making me watch TV, the Penelope and the Ed in me are very loud so the permission from an external source to give me grace helps me tremendously.

Perhaps this could be a useful tool for you as well. Let your loved ones in and advocate for yourself. I am allowing you, right now, to be your own friend and do something that you want to do. In fact, I am not only giving you the go-ahead, but I'm encouraging it. And if it helps you, great!

☙ K C ❧

Uncertainty

I'm embarking on this chapter without a title or even a topic. I have an urge to write (and not journal) because of all the pent up emotions coursing through me. I woke up nauseated. I am quite frankly angry at dickhead Ed right now. Angry that he still has his talons sunk into my extraordinary daughter. Angry that, try as I might to just live in the moment, I don't see an end in sight. There is definite progress—yet I see the areas where there is room for improvement and bile starts to rise, scorching my throat. I so very often feel like I'm not good enough to be this constant source of support for Bryn. I know that I cringe when she tells me she's always had this underlying feeling of not being good enough which drove her towards her dang perfectionism to begin with. Most times I don't try to figure out where that stems from (again, living with the mantra: "it is what it is") but it's hard not to wonder if I somehow caused that trait. But boy can I relate to that feeling of not measuring up, at this very moment. I'm questioning everything I do—or don't do. I know I'm supposed to challenge Bryn more with varieties of fear foods, yet I have fallen into the trap of serving her safe foods because I want to give her a reprieve from the constant hell and torment that Ed puts her through. I often feel that so much of life is a compromise and that if she's getting the nutrition, with food alone being such a struggle, that really is a small step towards victory. Yet, on the other hand, if I'm allowing Bryn to only eat what's "comfortable" to her, I'm letting that jerk Ed win. Time and time again, I feel I'm at the end of my rope. Many of Bryn and my arguments stem from neither of us feeling we're doing a "good enough" job.

Some of Bryn's daily homework is to read or say positive affirmations. I think I need to incorporate this more into my habits as well. As much as I do remind myself of the progress, I need to focus on the achievements even more. I tell Bryn that she needs to "mind fuck" herself and I must do the same. I am succeeding in the sense that I have lovingly fed her and restored her weight, we are so close to being on a maintenance plan. So, why am I feeling that because she's not eating enough variety, that's not good enough? We're teaching Bryn self-compassion, another thing I-myself need to work on. I hate that Bryn is such a perfectionist as I firmly believe that perfectionism is one of the greatest forms of self-abuse; yet, here I am expecting myself to be the greatest, most flawless mother of all times, EVER. And I'm falling short. Of course, I am because there's no such thing as perfect. I am more than human. I've lost my patience, lost my temper, said things I can't take back. Then I beat myself up severely because I've always been my harshest critic. Did Bryn learn these awful self-abusive behaviors from me? I have worked my tail off over my entire life to build my self-esteem and practice self-love and for the most part, I feel I've somewhat mastered it. Subsequently, Ed entered the picture with all of his cruel tests and has thrown me back into self-doubt.

I think one of the hardest parts of all of this lately has been how lonely it has been and continues to be. It feels as if we are in this prison, battling this horrible demon with hardly anyone even knowing. The handful that are aware of the situation, will check in occasionally but I'm sure they feel very uncertain as to how they can be of any help. I still don't know how to answer people who ask "what do you need?" because no one else can battle this besides Bryn and I. There isn't another soul present for the endless meals, tears, and struggles. I'm too exhausted after fighting Ed day in and day out to even contemplate getting out and doing something with friends. I find myself secretly wishing more and more that I had a companion to share in the adversity. If nothing else, someone to hold my hand and reassure me that it will be ok. I remember on day one of Bryn's treatment, other parents were at the hospital as it was their seventeen-year-old daughter's first day as well. The mother stayed behind and her husband, as he was leaving to go to work; kissed her goodbye and thanked her for all she was doing for their family of seven. There was such love and respect in his words, actions, and eyes. It was truly a heartwarming thing to witness but then it was replaced by a pang of envy. Since my divorce six and a half years ago, I've chosen to be single so there's no complaining about that now. This is the life that I've been put on Earth to live, therefore I must make the best of it. It is a journey that is just so fucking, overbearingly lonely sometimes. Rant over. I guess this was more like a journal entry. Oh well, writing is writing and is often very cathartic.

❧ BRYN ❧

The Alternative

I use my funeral as a motivator.

Sounds pretty dark but let me explain before you chalk this statement up to just that.

During the times that felt the most horrific and excruciatingly exhausting, despite my determination, I would cry into my mom's lap and declare my surrender: "I'm giving up. I can't do this anymore." And my mom would stroke my hair and gently pose the question, "What's the alternative?"

Each time this happened, and boy did these fits happen quite often (anywhere from once a week to even twice per day on the worst days), my brain would forget about this question so my mom would ask it again and again. And, as moms usually are, she was right. My alternative was dying. Letting Ed win and have the final say meant digging my own grave. Ed would have pushed me to the point of death.

So when I think of going back to Ed or giving up the fight towards recovery, I think of all the people that would be dressed in black with wet cheeks silently listening to my family and loved ones reading my eulogy while sharing stories and memories about me. I think about my friends, my extended family, my chemistry teacher, my guidance counselor, my therapists, my coaches, my peers that I smile at in the hallway, the ones who've had a falling out with me, my ex-boyfriend's family (whom I'm still very close to), the little kids I've babysat, my second family and practical brothers, my parent's friends, my brother's friends who always say hello to me when they see me in public or come to pick my baby bro up from our house, my pup and kitten, my old bosses and co-workers, my friends in other states. All of the lives I've touched through extracurriculars, the strangers that I have made laugh, families who have kids that attend my school. I think of my brother growing up without a sister to tell all his adventures to, and especially my mom's heartbreak if I were to be gone.

It's easy to forget how many people you affect without thinking twice about it. We've all heard the stories of someone planning to commit suicide and another showing them the smallest yet most sincere act of kindness such as help carrying school books or striking up a conversation. That simple act that saved their lives may have been by someone that they didn't even know.

Yesterday my friend got a flat tire by hitting the curb on the way to our Sunday ritual of seeing a $5 movie. After the movie, my two seventeen-year-old friends and I went to change her tire in the parking lot. Well, you can imagine how changing a tire might go when it entails three seventeen-year-old girls who had never changed a tire before.

A family drove up in a very nice BMW and parked two spots away from my friend's car. Instead of going in with his family and dismissing the teenage girls hysterically rolling a tire around the Toyota Camry, the dad and driver of said gorgeous BMW asked if we needed some help. Not wanting him to miss his movie, we told him that he could go in, but this kind man refused. He spent his time changing my friend's tire and telling us that he gets it because he hit a curb in high school, too, rather than picking movie seats with his kids and wife.

This man probably had no idea how much of an impact he made but with the challenges each day poses for me at this point, any act of kindness is a true godsend.

My point being, there are strangers and acquaintances who are touched by your very presence and life too. Whether you just say good morning to another person walking their dog or tell the cashier at Walgreens to have a nice day or compliment someone's appearance, it may change the course of their whole day. If you didn't exist or weren't able to provide those small acts, the domino effect could quite possibly happen in a backward motion. But lives are affected by you. People would be saddened to know of your death because you matter far more than your eating disorder tells you that you do.

So, I use my funeral as a motivator. I have to eat because I don't want my French teacher to cry when she hears I've passed away. I have to eat because I don't want strangers to feel sick because they read the news story of a 17-year-old's premature death. I have to eat because I have people that make me smile and people to provide a smile to in return. I have to eat because I have to live. But most importantly, I have to eat because I want to live.

⚘ K C ⚘

Grieving your now changed loved one

Something, or perhaps I should say one of the *many* things, I was unaware of when I first embarked on this journey was that anorexia and the recovery would completely change the baby girl that I had known since birth. There are no books or programs that prepare you for this. One of the hurdles I've encountered is my own grief of who she used to be.

Bryn had always been such a reasonable, logical child. I remember her at just two years of age, mastering concepts that most toddlers couldn't. For example, she'd explain clearly to me why it was dangerous to run out into the street. At two! And she never did run into the street. Or at three, after her baby brother had been born; I used to call her my lady bug and Cameron my bumble bee. Well, one day she says: "Mommy, bumble bees are bigger than lady bugs but I'm bigger than Cameron." There's no arguing with that logic so from then on, she became my "butterfly" (which we know is bigger than a bumblebee) and to this day, she remains my beautiful butterfly. What I didn't know back then was that at seventeen, that butterfly would have to endure such a painful metamorphosis. She is still fiercely smart and logical until matters of food, weight or body image come into play. At that point, all good sense goes right out the window, leaving us gaping—in horror sometimes—at the senselessness of it all and wondering "where is our Bryn?". The hardest part for all who know her is that she used to love food. As a baby, I made a lot of her baby food. I pureed various vegetables and then froze them in ice cube trays, popped them out and sealed them in breast milk bags, for whenever I needed them. I felt like such an accomplished mom, getting her palate accustomed to all sorts of different foods. It's debilitating for me at times to see her dread and fear of food now. Just last summer, she and I would go and try new restaurants and share each other's food. I really miss being able to eat out. I'm a pretty decent cook too and my kids have always raved about how good my meals are. They never wanted to be invited to Thanksgiving dinner elsewhere because they wanted my cooking. I miss hearing those words out of Bryn's mouth: "great meal mom". Will I ever hear them again? With the warmer weather, we used to eat out on the back deck but that's outside of Bryn's comfort zone right now. Another thing that I miss.

Upon entering the six week program, we thought we were just battling 'the' eating disorder. At that time, we had no idea that anorexia was a direct symptom of Bryn's anxiety, perfectionism and lack of true sense of identity. Well, that can of worms has been opened. She is fighting so bravely with this new normal. Situations that she never blinked an eye at all her previous years of life, such as her brother's sports games, now cause her overwhelming anxiety. She's always been adept in social situations. She was the type of baby to be able to sleep through a loud wedding then grew up to adapt to any situation. Looking back, however, with the knowledge I have now; I see some things that could have been indicators. As a baby, she had big time separation anxiety, for example, she didn't like being held by anyone but me. This did last longer than some but everything I read, put me at ease and she did outgrow it. Then, as a toddler, she didn't like the "in your face" type kids. Those that had lots of energy and were loud or brusque. She outgrew that as well, or so I thought. I suppose she just learned to adapt to the best of her abilities and quite possibly just push those anxious feelings down. Was I wrong to reassure her that it's ok, did that actually send a message to her that it was wrong for her to feel that way? Who knows. I do know that constantly trying to figure out if I did things wrong and how I could have possibly done them differently isn't going to change what has transpired. So, instead, I try to remind myself that it's on and forward. As the saying goes: "there's a reason your windshield is bigger than your rearview mirror".

My fourteen-year-old son misses the *old Bryn* terribly, he has told me this on numerous occasions. He doesn't know how to handle this huge change. He has continued to want to live with his father because it's too hard trying to adjust to the never ending roller coaster. The moods and emotions can be all over the place from being withdrawn to angry to anxious to fits of tears. It is difficult, especially since for years, outwardly,

Bryn had us all fooled with this sense of confidence. She had it all together. She was this perfect student, volunteered at the hospital, auditioned and booked television commercials, did dance, was part of National Honor Society, and the list goes on. She was always so busy but handled it all well and claimed to like it that way. Cameron has always looked up to her, idolized her even. He still does but it's so scary for him to see her in such a vulnerable state. I finally had to explain to him that I know he misses his sister but that we may never get that version back. All her "bubbly-ness" back then was a facade masking such deep anxiety. That's not to say she won't be happy and bubbly again but this has forever changed her. And us.

I urge you to give yourself some slack if you go down memory lane and think of how happy your loved one "used to be". Allow yourself to grieve but know that this journey of recovery is making them that much stronger and they will come out of this a better version of themselves. Adversity is a great teacher. I know that is one of the only things that keeps me going sometimes. Hold on to that precious hope because it is a long and rocky road, but one that in the end will build them up and help them to find their truest identity by shedding the one that they've taken on: ED.

My Bryn's Poetry

i'm sorry, mommy
i'm sorry i couldn't eat for you today
it doesn't mean i don't love you
i just couldn't open my mouth and chew
it's not that i picked the devil over you
well i did but i didn't mean to
so i'm sorry, mommy
because you were always enough
i'm sorry i couldn't do it for you

–a ghost's poem if I kept living like i was

i'm sorry, baby brother
i'm sorry i died today
you did not deserve to feel my heart cease to beat
i didn't mean to leave you sister-less
best friend-less
surrounded by people but utterly alone
i love you, baby brother
my spirit will never leave your side
even when you yell and cry
even when i slice into your thoughts when someone mentions the reason
even when you're numb and the pain is anything but poetic
i will give you my light
rub your back and kiss your cheeks
though you won't know it
because i will be bodiless

−the reason i eat

i'm sorry, my friend
i'm sorry you couldn't get out of bed long enough for my casket to be branded in
your nightmares
i didn't foresee the dying young they speak of
i'm sorry i left you early
i couldn't meet your children
ours would have had grand play dates
i left your cup without a drop and only the memories to haunt you
i'm sorry i missed your wedding
i'm sorry i missed your 21st
your 40th
your 75th
but most of all, i'm sorry your tears could not save me

−i will not die from this

You can imagine the wind being knocked out of me when I read this poetry. It shattered my heart and knotted my stomach but I knew that it was part of Bryn's process. Those words, she needed to feel them and getting them out, poetically, onto paper, was cathartic. The proof? We're years removed from those poems and she's still here, not having to apologize. She is thriving.

❦ KC ❦

More on grief

So much could be written on this subject as I have suffered such a variety of losses (death, endings, betrayals, etc...) over my lifetime already—as most I'm sure have. As much as I feel I understand it, I'm not entirely always comfortable embracing it when it pops up. And boy, does it still like to rear its ugly head often in my life.

Last night, during dinner, Bryn admitted to me that had I not caught on to her eating disorder when I did, she had predicted she would have quite possibly died within four months since her restriction became fierce overnight. Although we are many months out of program and in recovery, that statement sucker punched me and tears immediately sprang to my eyes. I still find myself grieving at the possibility of her death.

She has been writing a lot of poetry lately and a few of them were from the perspective of her dying. In essence, they were apologies to me, her brother, her loved ones after succumbing to Ed. Again, bile rises and burns at that thought and I truly get thrown into a deep sadness that gets confused with grief. I simply cannot allow my thoughts to go there as I deeply feel that I wouldn't survive that. I have gone all in with this recovery and refuse the possibility of Ed still finding a way to win down the line. Bryn has far too much to live for. She is so talented in many areas: acting, art, photography, singing, writing, she's smart, has an incredible sense of humor, a kind heart, the list goes on. She can and will take on the world by the balls, if it's the last thing I see to. I've grieved enough already and refuse to even contemplate grieving over my beautiful first born child. Period.

Then, at times, I also grieve over my former care-free self, the woman I was before becoming a care-giver and food-enforcer. Times were simpler when I thought I could trust that basic needs would be met, such as nutrition, in case I wasn't around for whatever reason. In the last few months I have given Bryn more freedom to go do things with her friends or boyfriend but am always on edge, asking her what she ate and when. It feels like I am an overbearing mother. We are both having to adjust to this *new* me. I know I've written about how Ed changes us all, this is yet another example.

But as with all loss, there are also new beginnings even if adjusting to them is initially tough.

❦ BRYN ❧

My values vs. Ed's values

Though Ed is in me, Ed and I are very separate people. Well quite honestly, Ed isn't a person at all. He's a monster— a vicious, blood-sucking black blob piece of shit, which is why my mom nicknamed him Dickhead Ed. I know that by naming him, I'm giving him an identity but that serves a purpose for defeating him in the end.

Because we are different—as contrasting as the devil and angel that sit on shoulders and whisper into people's consciousness—it is quite obvious our values are opposite. My therapist during Program asked me to do an exercise— no, not that kind of exercise, not physical exercise—. This involved writing down all of my values and seeing which of them Ed had manipulated or destroyed.

I'll give you a few examples. Bryn values honesty first and foremost as well as trust, loyalty, love, time, service, balance, independence, friends and family, community, self-care, acceptance, and courage.

Now, these are the values as corrupted by Ed:

Honesty. I began lying to my friends and family as well as to myself on behalf of Ed. I made my brother lie for me to keep my secrets of how little I was eating. Ed and I were not honest in our relationship, and what is a relationship without honesty?

Friendship. I wouldn't eat with my friends when they went out to restaurants and I didn't participate if they wanted to go get ice cream. I would tell them that I had already eaten.

Gratitude. I wasn't grateful for food or that my mom took the time to make meals because I would just throw them away.

Accountability. Ed and I constantly made eating disorder excuses. Ed and Edward the Excuse Maker teamed up together to find any possible justification for my actions. Ed controlled what I was doing and saying.

Knowledge. Ed clouded my knowledge. I didn't believe I was sick or that I needed food. His lenses of my body were and still are not logical.

Peace and balance. My thoughts constantly were filled with calories, food, exercise, plans about how to avoid food or keep myself busy, along with several other eating disorder voices. I wasn't peaceful at all and because I cut out so many foods and activities due to Ed, my life was rigid, the complete opposite of balanced.

Family. The eating disorder flipped my family upside down. Before Program I had many mood swings and took it out on them. They got all of Ed's wrath. Through Program our lives were completely different and now we will never be the same.

Self-care and self-love. Though Ed made it feel like I was caring for myself, I severely damaged my organs and body. I made myself sick and didn't care for my health. Ed made me hate myself with the comments about how I look, creating a hatred toward myself.

Happiness. It's very clear that I was not happy in my relationship with Ed, though he tints the memories to make it seem like I was. He twisted the definition of happiness to fit his needs. I felt a high each time I skipped a meal, refusing nourishment for myself. I didn't like who I was or my appearance and now I'm even more unhappy having to be force-fed.

Acceptance. I didn't accept or believe I was sick because my love for Ed covered up my self-awareness. Ed didn't let me accept me for who I was until I got to the weight he wanted me at and was completely in control of my food intake.

Problem-solving. My judgment became completely distorted. I didn't think Ed was a problem so I didn't need to solve it. My rationale was, and still sometimes is, out the window.

Morals. Bryn lives by her morals but with Ed's influence, started hiding things, lying, ceased healthy communication, and let anger spew all over loved ones. Morals were no longer a priority because Ed was.

Freedom and Independence. I am not one person, at least I don't feel like I am. It feels as if there are two people inside of me, fighting to win control over my emotions, logic, health, morals, self-image, view of food/exercise, and fighting to take charge of my personality.

Humor. Everything regarding food, exercise, body image, societal standards, etc. became ultra-sensitive. There was a lot less laughter.

Respect. I didn't realize how disrespectful and uncaring Ed's view of me was. I didn't respect myself or others when I was preoccupied by the eating disorder.

Safety. I put myself in danger by making myself very sick. I damaged my organs and heart. I could have permanently caused my reproduction system to not allow me to have kids. I could have developed full-blown osteoporosis. I was not safe in my own skin.

Time. I didn't spend my time on the things I loved. All my time was devoted to my very needy other half. I only thought about food. The entirety of time in each day was engulfed by Ed. He was like black ink that seeped into every aspect of my life, staining my being and my interests.

This exercise helped me see how I am not Ed and I must continue to separate myself from the eating disorder. My values make up my identity and are endlessly important. When my therapist suggested it, I couldn't think of a single bad thing about Ed; I had no idea Ed had hurt my values this much until I got out a pen and paper and wrote it all down.

Ed doesn't get to be that black ink damaging my character anymore. I now have the most kick-ass stain remover.

Humor, Truly the best medicine

So often I recount the horrors and less pleasant aspects of this illness. It is surely draining and hard but I think that I'm able to stay somewhat sane with a healthy dose of humor. A pride I hold dear to my heart is that my kids and I know how to poke fun at ourselves or ridiculous situations in an attempt to lighten things up—or just survive them. The way I see it, if we must go through hellaciously painful moments, we might as well do it with some laughter. Do we have barrels of fun every day? No, not yet anyway. However, we do have moments where we can laugh and see the hilarity and absurdity of things. Laughing is one of my favorite audible expressions. The physiological responses alone are beneficial. It is proven to decrease stress hormones while increasing immune cells and antibodies and triggers endorphins that help in pain relief. Having suffered for years with chronic pain, I found comfort in knowing that author and journalist, Norman Cousins, was able to cure himself of a life-threatening disease of the connective tissue involving the degeneration of collagen. He chronicled his amazing recovery in an article in the New England Journal of Medicine called "Anatomy of an Illness (As Perceived by the Patient)". If you need more evidence of the power of full belly laughter, I urge you to research this remarkable story.

Back in Program, Bryn had just graduated to being able to have weekends out of the hospital. We had decided to go to the Denver Art Museum since Bryn has a true appreciation and passion for art. I had to pack a snack, thinking to myself how it was throwing me back to the days of having little ones. Once we had parked, I gave Bryn half of her snack, a banana and a juice and told her she could have the rest when we got back to the car which had been a Chewy granola bar—something only a year prior she'd eat as a snack almost on a daily basis. She had a complete fit the whole Interstate ride towards home (about a half-hour drive). I explained that she'd have to drink boost if she refused to eat. When she stated that she wouldn't, I proceeded to tell her that the friend that was scheduled to come over that evening wouldn't be able to. She mistook the repercussion for not prioritizing nutrition as a threat. She continued with her rant until finally she grabbed the granola bar (a mere 2 miles from the house) and proclaimed passionately: "just so you know, you are killing me with this granola bar that is filled with chemicals and GMOs, so when I'm dead, it'll be your fault, I hope you can live with that". I just burst out guffawing to a point of tears streaming down my face. It was so ridiculous and the drive home had been highly stressful that my release was to laugh. Initially, that made her even more mad until I said: "that was so funny, thank you for that. Was that Bryn or Ed talking?". She gave a half-hearted laugh and just like that, the mood had been lightened and the anger had subsided. Ironically, only a few days later, we were back at Children's hospital and had accidentally taken the wrong elevator in which an employee with a huge cart filled with boxes upon boxes of Chewy granola bars was riding up. I started to giggle as Bryn read my mind and glared over at me but with a smirk curling her lips. As he exited on the floor below ours, struggling to pull the cart out, a box of said granola bars shifted, plummeting and landing right at Bryn's feet. That was it, I lost it in a fit of uncontrolled giggles. When I was able to regain myself, I looked at her and simply stated: "The Universe sure does have a great sense of humor." To that, she shook her head but didn't deny it. Touchy subject, yes but she was able to see the serendipity of it and the humor in it.

A few days before Bryn was discharged from the hospital, my grandmother in France passed away. It had been an emotionally draining day for me. This thoughtful daughter of mine decided I needed a distraction that night and chose a movie for us to watch together. She had bought the movie Mr. Church with Eddie Murphy as a stocking stuffer for me for Christmas and we had yet to watch it, so that was her plan. The movie begins with Mr. Church cooking up a storm: all kinds of food, galore. We both laughed so hard at the irony. Had Bryn been triggered by it, she would have missed out on a lovely film, we both adored it.

Not long ago, Bryn and I came across a movie trailer for *The Road Within* about a man with OCD, another with Tourettes syndrome and an anorexic girl that all go on a road trip together. There was a part where the girl pokes fun at herself about thinking she's fat and states "I guess we all have our issues" right after the character with OCD, played by Dev Patel complains about his ritualistic behaviors interfering with daily life. It was actually pretty funny and Bryn could totally relate. Again, she could've been offended but instead saw the comicality of it. That light-hearted side of her just makes her that much more beautiful in my eyes.

When you're continuously fighting this battle to regain a semblance of a normal life, you can either focus on every negative phase or try to see the lighter moments where you can have some fun. I've often claimed that laughing sure beats crying. Humor is medicine. In this journey towards recovery, or with any hardship in life, really; it is authentically, a diamond in the rough.

❧ BRYN ❧

Ooh, more weight loss! She said sarcastically

You see, I've been at this for five months now, the whole recovery thing. I know in the grand scheme of things that really isn't a long time due to the fact that I know my full recovery will probably take years. I figured, though, at this point my body would be all fixed up and ready to go. Well, I was wrong.

My organs are still very sick and use up all the sources of energy I'm given each day. In Program, my mom made up a ton of ways to understand and explain to people the health effects that come with starving. How my mom put it during Program, in one of her brilliant metaphors, is that I'm like a plant. A plant, when it's extremely dry, slurps up any water it's given so quickly and then it's gone, already used up. My body is a plant— "slluurrppp." That's the sound effect we use when talking about why I need to eat so much; it usually makes me smile. That's also how I explained to my friends the reason I have to eat so much and so consistently. That analogy really helped them better understand. L, one of my sweetest and closest friends, sent me a photo of these cartoon plants and went on to tell me it made her think of me since my body needs the slurps. (She used the sound effect, hand motion, and all.)

Five months later, I'm still a dry and very under-watered plant. My body still takes all the nutrients in my food so quickly and efficiently that it just keeps wanting more. When I don't give it all the food it needs, I drop weight, hence the title of this chapter. Ed loves that I lose weight but with weight loss—because my meal plan and number on the scale are both watched so carefully and the fact that I still don't have food privileges over what goes into my mouth—my meal plan goes up which means eating more. Woohoo yes because that is exactly what Ed and I want. To eat more.

I have a lot of mixed emotions about losing more weight. Of course, my first instinct is to celebrate it and maybe I even feel a little bit of pride when my therapist tells me my weight has dropped. I still do not know the exact number of my weight and step on the scale backwards so I can't see the digits. I am however made aware if I go up or down and by how much. Having to eat more is the exact opposite of a celebration. It sucks. But I also know that I must have hurt my body and all of my organs pretty badly for them to still be needing so many nutrients. My therapist, Angela says it's hard on my body to keep fluctuating weight which means I constantly have to have a higher, more caloric meal plan.

At this point, when Angela says I'm down, it isn't a triumph. I have a hard time wrapping my head around how the heck I could lose weight when I'm eating so much and hardly exercising compared to what I used to. Edward the Excuse Maker says that walking around the mall doesn't count as exercise and I don't burn calories when I sleep which are both false and complete distortions. It all comes down to my body knowing what it needs and I, or my mom really, giving it that because if not I'll be stuck in the limbo of living and dying, healthy and unhealthy, which I don't think I want. Ed might want that but we already know that Ed is an abusive jackass. So the next time Ed says, "OOH more weight loss?" excitedly, I'll be putting him in time out.

❧ K C ❧

The never-ending "why I must eat?"

By now, you've presumably come to take in that the re-feeding process has quite literally become a full-time job. And an excruciatingly exhausting one to boot. Mealtimes become unexpected spectrums of emotions. Your child might feel anxious, tearful, angry, throw a complete temper tantrum (no matter their age), try bargaining, and the list continues… The question or should I say statement I often got was: "remind me again why I need to eat this."

I tried to keep my answers colorful as I was frankly becoming tired of my own broken record. I often felt that I was winging it. Seriously, I was no professional but fortunately was usually able to read Bryn's mood and therefore could typically appease her need for reassurance. (Exception here was during the anger stage which we'll discuss more at another time. That stage plain sucked. I could never, and I repeat, NEVER say anything right). Sometimes, she would be very satisfied with the breakdown of foods and how the nutrients were important for every cell in her body. At times, she wanted me to go further and explain that it transforms into energy or which organs benefited from what, such as the brains requiring fats—like a car needing oil. Every kid is different so I'm by no means suggesting that this type of information would be helpful to your child, specifically. I know that speaking with other parents and dietitians, those types of conversations were a big "no-no". Ultimately, you know your child/teen best. This is a journey with many trials and errors and to be completely honest, Ed is so unpredictable that sometimes the technique that you used just yesterday that worked marvelously, will blow up in your face two days later when you try to use it again.

One morning, I got this question again so I decided to go with another one of my analogies. I asked Bryn what would happen to a plant if we didn't water it for a very prolonged period of time. She said: "it would die…"

"True, but not right away." I answered and continued: "the dirt or soil would become extremely dry and start to crack and the leaves would start to droop and wilt. And what would happen if you gave it water?" She looked at me waiting for me to continue. "it would suck that water up faster than your eye could see." I stopped and made a slurping sound for emphasis. "So, you'd give it more water and 'schlup', it would suck it right up yet again." I paused with a smile and asked if she liked my wonderful sound effects (to which she laughed at me for being such a dork—but whatever it takes). I then proceeded with my conclusion: "You see, Bryn, that plant and soil is like your body. It was malnourished for a while and therefore needs more and more food. It's sucking it right up and that's why the meal proportions are getting bigger and your physical activity has been so limited. Your body is 'schlupping' all this vital nutrition." When I was finished, I could see in her eyes the understanding and relief. Small victory! I will take every little bit I can get because I never know when Ed will intrude with his ugly presence and fight my metaphors.

Another big tool that we've both been taught in therapy to combat the body image issues that drive the urge to restrict and the fear of weight gain is of course training the mind through thought challenges, but especially trying to give more credence to your life values (being happy, having good relationships where you can easily go out to eat with your friends, going off to College without this "monkey" on your back, one day being able to enter into motherhood, etc…) over the way you'd like your physical appearance to be. This is definitely a hard one that, like a muscle, needs to be used over and over again in order to gain strength. You have to practice it constantly before being able to master it. Bryn often gets mad at me when I tell her that she can choose to view something a certain way and retorts: "easier said than done, Mom!". I remind her that I never did say it was easy but that we most certainly have that beautiful gift of choice. And we are free to choose how to perceive things. I know that it sounds like a bunch of mind over matter mumbo-jumbo but I had started to embark on a journey of mindfulness years prior and knew without a shadow of a doubt that we humans are strong enough to reprogram our thinking. Again, I to this day continue to tell her that it's one of the hardest things she'll ever attempt and that she'll notice that most people don't even try because it is so difficult but that it is possible and to never give up—no matter how emotionally exhausted fighting Ed renders her.

❧ BRYN ❧

Nap Time

In Kindergarten, nap time is mandatory. Through grade school, middle school, and the start of high school, nap time was overrated and "for babies". Little did I know how often I'd be napping through my Junior year of high school.

While I was extremely undernourished from hardly eating anything, I spent a lot of spare time sleeping. Being the girl that would come home from school and do homework immediately without a break, having no fuel to energize my mind, I had to take a nap every day after school before I could think straight.

Fast forward to the days of Program. We would come home each night, shower, do night time snacks, and go to sleep immediately. Days were exhaustingly long. They were filled with overwhelming emotions, leaving us completely drained by the end of the day. Crying seven hundred times a day can really do a number on a person. Not to mention facing my biggest fear six separate times a day: food.

And now, out of Program, I still nap quite often. I used to use my nap as the "me" time my therapist assigned me to take. Until she told me that I in fact get a nap in addition to another hour of real me time. She said it's completely acceptable for my body to need extra sleep. The emotions were taxing by themselves and my body was also working hard to repair itself. Digesting is a lot of work for your body mostly since it hasn't had to do it for so long.

Penelope tells me naps aren't productive but she doesn't know how badly I need them. My body needs rest so I let myself sleep when I need it. I nap when I'm with my friends. I nap in the morning. I nap in the evening. I nap on the couch, on my bed, in my mom's room. I like my naps a lot. You should try it sometime.

❧ BRYN ❧

What do you do in your free time?

My friend brought me to a youth group. Isn't that how all great stories start? Anyway, the group leader came up to me and asked me to say three descriptive words about myself. I sat there staring at him totally blank because my first instinct was "ha well I'm anorexic!!!!!" Well, I was not about to say that. After I pulled three words out of my butt, he asked what I do in my free time. "Uhm I eat," went through my mind at first.

Over breakfast, I told my mom this story and we both laughed because of the accuracy! Honestly living this hell is awful enough so we find things to laugh about in order to lighten up the mood, even just a little bit. Of course, we don't make fun of anorexia or eating disorders, but finding the appropriate humor can really change up the emotions behind it.

A few weeks ago, we were watching a trailer for the movie, *The Road Within*. The only reason I came across the movie was because I was looking up my man on google (Dev Patel) and saw he was in it. He played a severely OCD character and the two other main roles were an anorexic girl and a young man with Tourette's Syndrome and they pretty much all escape from the mental institution they're in to go on a road trip. It looks hilarious but that's beside the point.

The OCD patient (played by actor Dev Patel—who I'm in love with at this point) says in the trailer, "These stupid rituals take over everything," and the character who is anorexic proceeds to tell him, "Yeah well I think I'm fat. I guess we all have our issues." Though this was supposed to be a pretty serious moment in the movie, mom and I died laughing. We can laugh because that's exactly how I feel. It's just too relatable.

KC TILLMAN AND BRYN TILLMAN

I'm living this. Well, really, we're living this every day. I figure it's okay to laugh at what I'm going through with eating disorder things and to poke some fun at myself without it being mean. There's a line between jokingly putting yourself down and just plain laughing.

Ups, downs, breast cancer scare with a dash of break ups

Life is going to happen regardless of the fact that you may be in the midst of the fight of your life with Ed. About seven months into Bryn's recovery, I was told that I was at the age to get my first mammogram. Not working, I felt that at least I had the time to go get it done. I walked out of there with a spring in my step, relieved that it didn't hurt as bad as some say and knowing that it was just a routine, preventative thing that was now behind me. Well, the very next day, I received a phone call asking me to come back the following week as the test was *inconclusive*. A bombshell that I was not expecting whatsoever. Initially I felt angry and couldn't believe that with everything else going on, life could have dished out this crap on top of it all. I felt that the Universe was a big ole bully. I emailed my doctor asking for more information wanting to determine the urgency, but also to see if I could possibly hold off for another month since things were busy. I was in the middle of a nine-week training class for voice captioning for television, a job I was able to work from home. I preferred to wait to undergo additional imaging, if at all possible. The doctor called back right away stating her recommendation that I go in. They spotted some asymmetrical areas and wanted to do further testing. Bryn was away with a youth camp (a feat in itself that she was able to go away and have a taste of independence) and Cameron was spending time with his paternal grandmother who was visiting. I was most definitely not going to tell them because I didn't want them to worry. The entire week I worked at not catastrophizing along with altering any thoughts if fear tried to barge in. It was without a doubt a challenging week but with grace and the use of mindfulness, I got through it. I'm happy to say that freaking out would have been in vain and a waste of energy. The spots they had detected were merely lymph-nodes.

A week after that, Bryn's boyfriend of a couple of months broke things off. Being a touch older than she, he had enlisted in a boot camp for the Navy and knew he'd be leaving eight months later and was afraid of getting too attached. Her eating disorder was also tough to handle. Going into the relationship, Bryn was immediately straightforward with her demons and battles and he initially was accepting of it. It therefore was quite a blow when, out of the blue, he ended it. She had called me in tears asking me to come pick her up as she was too upset to drive. That drive was one of the longest for me. I blasted my music while praying I wouldn't get pulled over and slapped with a speeding ticket. I couldn't get there soon enough to hold my broken-hearted baby girl. How tough to witness your kid go through heart shattering experiences. Furthermore, the timing of it sucked, she didn't need to deal with that on top of everything else that she was combatting. But, again, such is life. Adversity will keep coming at you, no matter what is already on your overflowing plate. Yes, pun intended. The knocks are what shape you and help you to grow. Sometimes you just wish for a small reprieve but that is out of your control, so you have to roll with the punches and just ride that wave. I often tell Bryn that it's way more exhausting trying to swim upstream but I know that many adults can't even grasp that concept, so it's a lot to expect a seventeen year old to adopt such a philosophy.

One thing I know for sure is that life and painful experiences can be less devastating when you choose to have a broader perspective and give into acceptance. The thing is, I've had my fair share of hardships in life before learning acceptance of what is. It takes a lot of work and practice. I often wish I could just take that knowledge out of my own being and simply download the information into both of my kids, to make things less painful for them. Yet, I must recognize and accept that these are lessons that must be learned on their own. They're on their own paths, my walking alongside them and lending my support when they stumble is sufficient.

I guess that my biggest message here is that life will continue to throw you curveballs on your journey towards recovery, you need to trust that you do have the power and strength to handle them.

* Update: They got back together the next day.

** Another update: They broke up a few months later.

Edge Letter- July 21, 2017

Letter Written for the Financial Supporters of the Youth Group I'm a Part of. I was able to go on a trip with the youth group thanks to their contributions. C., my student group leader asked if I could take part in the monthly newsletter he sends to the financial investors of Edge youth group. He told me that it could be as personal or impersonal as I wanted but that it may be a good opportunity for me to unpack. What he meant by that is that each person has their baggage, their struggles, their conflicts, their shit. While in California, one night he carried in his Edge backpack all zipped up. It was extremely heavy. He had kids around the room try to hold it up and you could visibly see the strain this big bag had on people. He opened it up and pulled out a big rock. The big rock represented part of his story, a heavy part that weighed him down, a part that was filled with painful emotions and memories. While he kept pulling out these boulders from his pack, he told us his life story and unloaded his burden. By the end, the whole room was in tears, overcome with grief—yet inspiration and admiration of his strength and determination. After his backpack had been emptied and the contents sprawled across the floor he went on to explain that each day you are going to wake up with your experiences and your backpack weighing you down. Each day you have to unpack your bag. Each day you have a choice to lay the bag down or carry it with you.

With this letter I took the risk of being judged by strangers, of putting all of my vulnerability out into the public. But I did it to unpack and possibly educate others about my pack. It was worth the risk.

My story. Every seventeen year old, scratch that, every teenager up to this point in their lives has a different story with its own quirks, struggles, enlightenments. If you set these stories adjacent to one another and look at all the rough edges and the soft spots, you'll find that there isn't a way to compare these stories because they are all so individual. They all carry their own lessons; they help to shape the one who has lived it. Edge is a book of all these non-fiction chapters full of lives that have been lived for fourteen to eighteen-ish years. Each page has its own original makeup but they are all bound together in this big book of experience and this book includes laughs, tears, bonds, friendship, and connection. This book celebrates differences and personality and acceptance. This book is Edge.

My name is Bryn. I'm seventeen, now a senior in high school (scary how quickly time flies!) I started going to Edge in April after a pretty big turning point in my life. I had just been discharged from a six week program at the Children's Hospital that had put my life on hold and flipped my world, and my family's world, upside down. I suffer from anorexia, anxiety, depression, OCD tendencies, and pretty severe perfectionism. I'll try to keep my story short and sweet because if not, this will probably turn into a ten page essay on mental illness and the lonely world it traps you in.

I know how stigmatized mental illness is, especially something like an eating disorder. Most people jump straight to the conclusion of, "oh they aren't eating out of vanity because they want to be skinny," when in reality, that is a very insignificant part of the bigger picture. As a little girl, all the way back to elementary school and middle school, I remember having this strange relationship with food. I was constantly scared of it. When I was eleven or twelve I stopped eating sugar and my friends would make fun of me and taunt me with, "Bryn's on a sugar diet." As time went on I restricted more and more: seventh and eighth grade on top of the "sugar diet" I wouldn't dare touch fast food (especially Panda Express), ninth grade I stopped eating carbs, tenth grade I went vegan, eleventh grade I stopped eating all together.

Now let me explain why, because I did not stop eating just for the sake of not eating. Eating disorders arise when the right genetic factors are met by the perfect concoction of environmental factors and boom, some people develop an eating disorder. For example, I have alcohol addiction on both sides of my family contributing to my addictive personality. I am naturally a perfectionist with impossibly high expectations for myself. I have anxiety and OCD which causes a lot of feelings of being out of control. One of my parents had higher expectations of me than I did of myself, which says a lot. No matter what I did, in school, extracurriculars, work, etc., I was never good enough. My accomplishments needed to be better. Giving my all did not suffice. Moving on, when I became vegan, I became really obsessive about what I put in my mouth. I was obsessively counting calories, even to the point that I counted the few calories in my sugar-free *chewing gum and vitamins. My boyfriend of a year and I broke up. School was extremely stressful as I was in all advanced placement and honors classes. I had started working out at the gym almost every day and as time went on I began going for longer and longer, intensifying my workouts. I would joke that I was literally trying to run away from my problems. What people do not understand about eating disorders is that the guilt of eating, thinking of food, feeling hungry, not working out, running for only 45 minutes instead of an hour, etc. is so intense and painful that you need the guilt to stop. The wars in my head were so loud that I couldn't take it anymore. For six years I fought those wars from both sides: team logical Bryn and team the eating disorder. The only person I wanted to escape more than anything was myself but I was stuck in my skin. I was too exhausted to fight myself anymore so to quiet the unbearable guilt, I just stopped. Those with eating disorders associate appearance, eating, and weight gain with failure. I had so many feelings of inadequacy each time I ate because I felt those inadequacies in my everyday life. When I put food in my mouth, I felt like a disappointment. I felt disgusting and unworthy of love, acceptance, and a life.*

Fast forward, to when my mom noticed and was terrified that her baby girl was going to die. I truly didn't understand why she thought I would die. There was no connection in my head that I needed food to live or that I was sick. At all. It's an addiction— not eating. I felt powerful each time I skipped a meal. I felt in control of myself, my life, and my choices. For the first time in a very long time, I felt confident in myself and what I looked like. I felt happy and secure, unlike any euphoria I had felt up to that point. In reality, I was very sick. I developed bradycardia and my blood pressure was orthostatic. Toward the end of the program, my team (my therapist, psychiatrist, dietitian, and adolescent medicine doctor) determined that I'd had anxiety for my whole life but kept it under control with my perfectionism and then coped with it by not eating. This was surprising at first and left my mom and I wondering how we didn't realize that I had anxiety. Looking back, we have found all of these instances through my whole life where, yes, I was anxious but didn't know to identify it as anxiety.

Carrying on, when I was first admitted, I was pretty severely underweight. The doctors wouldn't let me see my weight so I don't know the number which is probably a good thing. I'm learning that numbers do not define who I am. Though my eating disorder tells me that my worth and value depends on my outward appearance, the number on the scale, I must counter that with knowing that who I am is so much more complex than a combination of digits. Who I am is my identity, my values, my beliefs, my likes/dislikes, my interests, my loved ones, my hopes and dreams, my mannerisms, my vices, my motivations, my experience. I am not my eating disorder, my anxiety, my depression. I am Bryn and that is enough.

Back to how Edge comes into my story… my best friend, A, had been going to Edge for about a year. I decided that I wanted to go. Fresh out of the program and trying to learn how to resume my life, I was extremely anxious all the time. My days consisted of multiple panic attacks and meltdowns at meals. So I went to Edge and hardly talked. Everyone was still nice and welcoming. About a rollercoaster of a month or so later, I went again with A, and our other best friend, L. This time I was in a much better place and I had an incredible time. I met a bunch of new people (which is one of my favorite things to do). We played games and joked around. I smiled and laughed without having to force myself. I met C, the leader, who cracked me up and welcomed me into this group. I felt like maybe I had found a place where I could belong.

Two weeks before July 10, the day Edge was leaving for Biola University in California, I approached C to see if there was any possible way I could go even though it was so last minute. By some miracle I was able to get on that plane with my best friend and take a trip, the first real taste of independence in six months. My mom, with whom I live, has been out of a job so that she's able to take care of me. It was practically impossible, financially, for me to go on this trip but C made it happen. We made it happen and I am eternally grateful that I was able to attend. The week was full of challenges: anxiety attacks, feeling emotionally drained, and of course, eating independently. A. knew that I had to eat exactly what she did so my mom, therapist, A., C, and I had Plans A–Z ready to go before even driving to the airport. More importantly, though, the week was full of overcoming adversity, bonding, smiles and giggles with these new people in my life, creating memories, swimming in the ocean (and almost drowning a few times), learning how to accept who I am and my story, connecting with other people's vulnerability, and feeling inspired. I feel that this trip was part of my evolution, part of my road to recovery.

I am a firm believer that everything happens for a reason and there are no coincidences in the master plan of each of our elaborate lives. I don't believe me stumbling into C's life was accidental. I don't believe becoming a part of the Edge family and including my chapter in the book of our experiences was a mishap. I feel unbelievably fortunate to be intertwined in something bigger than me. I have met people who have touched me and I can only hope the same was reciprocated to them. For me, that is what life's all about: touching other's lives and evolving in your own being.

Lastly, I want to thank you for supporting something that is a safe place for teenagers. Thank you for supporting Edge because without you and the scholarship for this trip, I'm not too sure how we could have done it. And a world without Edge, well how sad would that be?!

All my love,
Bryn Tillman

P.S. Congratulations if you made it through that whole letter! I know I talk quite a bit so thank you for reading! ☺

❦ K C ❧

Journal entry 7/21/17

Back to reality and this eating disorder.… Bryn has stated for a few weeks now that Ed is louder than he's ever been. Louder than when she was in Program. All she wants to do is starve herself. That's such a hard one to hear. I don't necessarily know how to help her. I try to teach her acceptance of what is, countering the negative thoughts, positive affirmations, mindfulness, etc… basically all the tools I have acquired in my life that continue to really help me. But I sometimes wonder if she is capable of learning them. I tell her that I do know how hard it is and that it takes continuous practice, which then lets it come more naturally.

I'm having a hard time because when Bryn is feeling so yucky within herself, she tries to pick a fight with me in order to get her anger out. I know that is human nature but I don't know how many times I've said that I'm simply done being a punching bag. She will completely twist what I'm saying into something ugly. I've learned to really weigh what I'm saying carefully, yet, I say one thing and she hears something else; as if it went through the whole "Egyptian telephone" game. That is beyond frustrating. It, at times, makes me want to never say a thing to her. Right now, Ed is in total control of Bryn and he's such a mean jerk. Because he feels like I'm the enemy (because I make Bryn eat), I get a face full of rantings and don't even recognize my Bryn… I have to say, it gets really old being treated like I'm the enemy. Why can't she recognize that and turn her anger towards Ed, who ultimately deserves that anger as it's that part of her that has caused all this anguish? Could it be because she doesn't want to lash out at a piece of her very own being? I don't know. All I know is that I want to move to the next level of conquering this stupid ass eating disorder. This test of endurance is exhausting.

As Bryn inches more and more towards adulthood (she'll be 18 in less than 6 months), I need her to take on more responsibility and accountability towards food and her recovery but no matter how gently I hint at that, she lashes out and only hears that I think she's not good enough and not progressing enough which is NOT what I'm saying.

As I practice more and more of my own mindfulness, I'm coming to the realization that as much as I'm fighting for her not to die, ultimately, I have no control over that. She will eventually be on her own, move away and have to fight her own battle without me. I have to accept that. I try to stay in the present moment, as we're not there yet, she will remain here with me for at least another year…

I just feel like every fight we have, cracks a little bit more our strong foundation and that hurts me to no point.

Must run to get breakfast ready. My life: food.

❧ BRYN ❧

To the bone

In the midst of my recovery, Netflix released a movie that I find to be very offensive and frustrating. I haven't watched it because I know how triggering that would be for me at this point but I've read countless reviews, talked to friends about it, and watched the trailer. So, I decided to write to Netflix.

LETTER TO NETFLIX - JULY 29, 2017

Hello Netflix,

I feel as a customer of your company and a member of this community and society, it is imperative for me to speak up for myself and take the leap in order to allow my voice to be heard. I feel as someone who has experienced this life first hand, it is my duty to educate those around me.

I would like to speak with you about the Netflix Original, "To the Bone" that was released recently. As a seventeen-year-old who struggles with anorexia, I would like to address some concerns of mine regarding the film. First, let me share a quick and very condensed version of my story. At the beginning of this year, after years of restricting my diet, over-exercising, and grasping at straws to avoid the guilt of putting food in my mouth, I was hospitalized for six weeks at an eating disorder program. After being discharged, I have had a rollercoaster of a recovery with tremendous ups and downs. Currently, I eat to live. I eat because I do not want to die. I eat because I do not want my loved ones to spiral into a depression after burying me. I do not want to eat, but with major support from my mom (who creates my meal plans, makes meals for me, and watches me eat), my therapist, my dietitian, and my angels of friends, I eat to keep my heart beating.

I am a television, on-camera actor so I understand the ins and outs of the industry and can somewhat appreciate that this movie was made in order to shed light on eating disorders. Now let me tell you about my feelings on "To the Bone." I was completely sick to my stomach reading reviews on Netflix's new release. It infuriates me to think that so many girls and boys are going to be watching this movie, glamorizing an eating disorder. I remember watching eating disorder stories on YouTube while in the midst of restricting, utterly rapt by how badly I wanted to be like them. I thought it was beautiful to have the strength to stop eating. I idolized them. I glamorized it. I wanted to feel in control, feel powerful, feel like for once in my life I was good enough, that I had done something right. I wanted to be skinny because that is how I thought I could be accepted and lead a successful life. That is how I thought the wars in my head of guilt and inadequacy would cease-fire. I needed to quiet the unbearable emotions. I remember looking up ways to stop eating—which this movie gives plenty of ideas.

It enrages me that, though Lily Collins struggled (and most likely still struggles) with an eating disorder, she was required to lose weight to play the role of Ellen. From someone who has an eating disorder and who has been educated by several health care professionals, I would like to have you know that there is no such thing as "healthy weight loss" when someone is at their healthy body weight. Not only that but there is absolutely no way that someone who has recovered from anorexia can lose weight in a healthy manner. Not only is it extremely hard on the physical body, but it is monstrously hard on the emotional state. Having to lose weight for the role of Ellen could so easily have sent Collins into a relapse.

More importantly, if I understand correctly, I believe the purpose of this movie was to create an authentic portrayal of eating disorders but really, I feel that "To the Bone" just intensifies stigmatizations that eating disorders have a certain outward appearance. Casting someone as beautiful as Collins to play a role like this gives yet another perfect example of the stigma that eating disorders only affect white, vain, beautiful females though in reality, eating disorders do not discriminate against race, gender, weight, etc. Young girls and boys could easily fall into an obsession with eating disorders, dieting, and weight loss after watching this triggering film. It provides viewers with so many ideas on eating disorder behaviors (calorie counting, the provocation of comparing the most successful eating disorder and amount of times being in a program, etc.). If Lily Collins had been kept at the weight she was already at in order to play the role, it could have opened viewer's eyes to the reality that many times, those suffering from an eating disorder are at a weight that outwardly looks healthy though inside, their organs, bones, heart, and mental state are all very ill. Eating disorders, a lot of the time are an invisible illness because usually, struggling with an ED can not be seen with the naked eye. Collin's appearance is yet another stereotype that you must be a certain weight to be classified as having an eating disorder. For me personally, and many of the friends that I met through the program I was in, I constantly made ED excuses about how I wasn't skinny enough to have an eating disorder or I wasn't unhealthy enough to have an eating disorder when in reality, I was very sick and developed bradycardia and an orthostatic blood pressure among other things. This unrealistic movie emphasizes that false stigma when we should be trying to change that.

Continuing on, I understand how for publicity purposes, comedies are intriguing but I'm very offended by the fact that this movie was originally listed as a comedy because there is absolutely NOTHING funny about living life with an eating disorder or witnessing a loved one struggling to do the one thing they need to do to survive: eat. I must say that I am repulsed by Hollywood's inauthentic portrayal of what this life consists of. I find it very triggering each time I log onto Netflix and the first movie that appears in the spotlight and popular movies and recently added is "To the Bone." This is still a very sensitive topic for me and for many in my life. In a dream world, I wish for this movie to be taken off Netflix so that no ED recovery is damaged any longer by this movie as well as preventing others from falling into dangerous eating disorder habits. If this is not feasible, I would like to request for Netflix to at least remove "To the Bone" from the spotlight.

I appreciate the time you have taken to read my concerns. Thank you.

Bryn Tillman (Denver, CO)

Not a choice

I want to make it quite clear that having an eating disorder is not a choice. It is a perfect concoction of genetic makeup and environmental factors that boom, blossom into and eating disorder. Some people clearly don't have an eating disorder which is why it takes just the right puzzle pieces to develop one.

Even years before my eating disorder became full-blown, I had many ED thoughts. The thoughts over the years became stronger and louder, exploding my guilt and belittling myself. I felt guilty if I ate anything at all but especially larger portions, sweets, or any of the foods Ed deemed as "bad". I felt guilty if I didn't work out every day or if I failed to suck in my stomach while sitting. I felt guilty if I didn't follow Ed's rules to perfection because he said I was a failure.

The guilt became unbearable. The pressure of not being good enough in Ed's eyes, in my own eyes, no matter what I ate or did was oppressive. To avoid the guilt, the lack of control, the feelings of inadequacies, I stopped it. I needed to escape the screams in my head and the waves of guilt tumbling under pounds of rushing water. I stopped eating because if I didn't eat, the guilt was lessened, I felt successful, like I had greatly achieved, and I had complete control over anything that I put in my body.

As you find reliable resources on anorexia, it becomes much clearer that the illness is not about the food. The feelings of failure, need for control, management over anxiety, craving for perfection, were all cured (in hindsight, falsely cured) by starvation. Feeling fat is not about weight. Lucy Howard-Taylor in her book Biting Anorexia says it best: "The idea of 'feeling fat' is just the symbolic underlying feelings. I finally realized what I was feeling: unmanageable, bloated, queasy, confused, fearful, worthless, unhappy, distended, and lonely. And somehow my brain translated all that into one word: fat."

It is my choice, however, to reach out for help if I feel unable to battle the ED thoughts alone or have had a slip. It is my choice to want to recover and to kick Ed out of my life.

⚘ KC ⚘

Forever changed in
so many ways

Ed slowly crept into our lives and then rapidly set up residence. I must admit, I have changed so much as a person. Obviously Bryn has as well and so has Cameron. We've all become ultra sensitive to certain comments regarding food or weight. I know that I used to laugh at some posts on Facebook such as "I went for a jog this morning and heard a lot of clapping before realizing the sound was from my butt cheeks slapping together". Those things no longer make me laugh, it's sad actually. I know I'm still new to this journey but for example, this morning, I had to take Bryn to school because it had snowed and she didn't want to clean the snow off her car and I didn't really want her driving. On the return drive home I was listening to the morning radio and they were joking about the worst foods to try and eat while driving. I didn't think much of it but turned the station to one where they were discussing all-you-can-eat buffets which led to them talking about eating contests and my stomach just churned. I often tell Bryn that she will need to develop a thick skin and to let those types of conversations roll off her back as food and exercise are incessant societal subjects of conversation. I've explained that it's similar to someone being raped and then hearing people constantly talking or joking about sex; that would be extremely uncomfortable, yet it is a part of life. I suppose I'm going to need to take my own advice here.

I've also lost some weight recently with all of this. Partly due to stress but also because I'm eating more often now so Bryn doesn't feel she has to eat alone. I believe the several meals/snacks have bumped up my metabolism. When I see people I haven't seen in awhile, they have no qualms mentioning that I've lost weight and immediately ask how I did it. It is excruciatingly uncomfortable for me. Something that is given as a compliment, I wince at because it reminds me every single time that our society is so focused on people's appearances. Did I not look fine with the extra pounds? Am I only worthy of compliments now that I'm "thin enough"? It really is a hard one to swallow when I have a daughter with anorexia at home. I just want to scream: "Can we NOT talk about physicality?!" I think the hardest part for us is when it's an actual family member that just doesn't get it. Not that they don't want to but they don't think ahead of what they are saying. Or they feel they are entitled to be able to pass judgment, because, well… they're family.

Cam tells me he gets very uncomfortable as well when his female friends talk about being fat or what not. This eating disorder has affected us on so many different levels, it's astonishing. As a mother, I feel it has changed me on a cellular level. I know we must continue to push through, and we will. I just didn't expect this to be such a life changer. I guess it's part of adjusting to this new—and hopefully temporary—normal.

Eat 6x, Rinse and Repeat

"Bryn, you ready for breakfast?" "Come have a juice please." "Okay, I'm going to go make lunch." "I need you to eat a snack before you go." "Dinner will be ready in five." "I'm going to get your snack." Every day. Every single day. This is the routine and it's a lot. Usually I have the same breakfast, similar variations of lunch, and the same night time snack. I'd say breakfast is the easiest at home because I know what I'm having and it lessens my anxiety. If the plans change, though, and I'm presented with a different breakfast, Ed throws a fit.

I know food is my medicine and I have to eat it to regain my health. Six months later and my organs are still not healthy enough to be eating "normally". My hunger cues are still nonexistent for the most part. Mom and I will have a practically identical breakfast and a few hours later she'll claim to be hungry when I still feel full. It's quite frustrating having to eat when you're constantly full but my body needs it and my weight shows when I don't get all the nutrition I need. This doesn't mean it's not exhausting. It is. This morning at breakfast I told mom how it gets old having to eat so often every single day.

My sweet friend, Nicole, suggested to me one day after a difficult lunch out that I could just think of each day as a checklist. Lunch, check. Now only two snacks and one more meal to go. As I was still feeling frustrated, anxious, and discouraged, I responded with, "Yeah but then the checklist is erased every day and I have to do it all over again. I don't get anywhere." It's practically a never ending cycle. Nicole said to me without missing a beat, "Stop future tripping." And she was right. Future tripping is the phrase we say when you are so worried about the future or are too focused on looking ahead that you can't enjoy the present. You want to avoid future tripping so that you can live in the moment without anticipation of what will come. Future tripping disrupts your present.

I stopped future-tripping and thought about how right she was. Instead of looking at eating as a chore, I can think about it as an accomplishment every time I take my last bite and finish a meal. I have to remind myself that every day is a new day which is filled with new opportunities, not solely more food. I have to take my medicine everyday but that is just part of my life, how I have to live. I take it one meal at a time. Check. On to the next check box. Acceptance sure makes the pill easier to swallow.

❧ K C ❧

Beating a dead horse

I realize what a gruesome title for a chapter this is. But I just can't think of a better analogy when I'm going over the same feelings about this dang eating disorder month after month. I know that I referenced the movie "Groundhog Day" explaining our days in program, the emotions that are attached to this life changing event are quite similar as well. You work your tail off in therapy to let go of expectations and accept where you are in the process of recovery, when out of the blue, you are winded by the suddenness of frustration that just seemed to have barged in from nowhere. Yet it doesn't just come from nowhere, you see, no matter how hard you're working on it, you are just like the sufferer/patient in the sense that you can be triggered by things as well.

I am a big time over-thinker. What I mean isn't that I necessarily over analyze things, yet, my mind feels as if it is in perpetual motion. Sometimes it is busy with the most trivial thoughts. I'm not curing disease or coming up with the next formula or equation to solve quantum mechanics, no, I'm not smart enough for that. When I say I overthink, it's that there is never a time that I don't have something going through that thick skull of mine. Maybe it has partly been due to the fact that being single for so many years now, I have learned to enjoy my own company and fill my mind. I'll go down memory lane or if I'm driving, I might look over at a passenger in another car and wonder what their lives are like. I'll think about a book I've been reading or a television show or movie I just saw. I'll imagine the life of my dreams and get lost in that fantasy world. And then I pull myself back to reality–– but sometimes, for a split second, that reality doesn't include an eating disorder. That reality is "pre-Ed diagnosis" and I'll have a thought such as: "Maybe I can surprise the kids and take them to a nice restaurant for dinner." for whatever occasion. Then, BAM true reality catches up. I get thrown for a loop and just like a person suffering from mental illness can get triggered, I am triggered, rendering my mood to crap.

All the yucky emotions that bubble up from anger to frustration to sadness typically tend to end with the same emotion: grief. I miss being able to celebrate with food. I miss hearing Bryn excited over eating something. I miss being able to go out to eat on a whim. I miss seeing her order food because it sounds good not out of fear of what it will do to her mental state or body. I miss (as does her brother— who mentioned it several times over the last holiday season) Bryn's amazing desserts, even though I'm not much of a desert person. Lastly, I miss not tensing up immediately with talk surrounding food or body image. I could go on... *That* is what I mean about beating a dead horse. Seriously, what good is it going to do? No sense crying over spilled milk, right? So, I allow myself to be butt-hurt for a while but then, as I've done with every other obstacle in life, I get up, dust myself off and remind myself that it's ok to miss those things. It's akin to missing nursing your babies or kissing your toddlers' boo boos. The reality is that those times are gone, they are in the past. There is no use dwelling on what is no longer. Instead, I am going to embrace where we are now, get excited over the milestones of recovery (such as Bryn trying a bite of something scary or getting herself to eat ice cream or going out to restaurants with her friends, or simply not crying over every meal like she did when she was first in program at the hospital).

Talk about rehashing, I know I keep repeating that the way to not go completely insane with worry or fear or anxiety is by staying present in this very moment. Not yesterday, not tomorrow. Now. I remember texting Bryn and her boyfriend who are in a long distance relationship this saying from the Dalai Lama on New Year's day: It said, "There are only two days in the year that nothing can be done. One is called yesterday and the other is called tomorrow, so today is the right day to love, believe, do and mostly live." Such wisdom. Had I not started incorporating mindfulness into my world a couple of years ago, I'm not sure I would have survived this life altering illness of Bryn's. I know it must seem redundant reading the same words about living one day at a time, but, I wholeheartedly believe that it is one of the keys to joy not only for all human beings but especially for those going through huge adversity. Those dealing with a chronic illness or those being caregivers have so much to gain from learning to train their minds to be in the NOW and to let go of all the what if's. Honestly, we have no control over tomorrow and worrying about what might or might not happen is helping no one. All it does is take away your precious peace.

I will finish by sharing what I tell my son when I am trying to help with life lessons—I impart this to Bryn as well but Cam has been the one needing my "pep-talks" lately. I voice with all the love and compassion in my heart: "This is by no means meant to be a lecture. I happen to have lived, it has been a rough life at times. If any of what I have learned can help to make it less painful for you, that is my ultimate goal. You have your own lessons but I'd like to prevent you from hurting as much as I have." With that being said, I am all too aware that we all have our own paths to walk, our own lives to live. But, if a simple piece of advice can help you to navigate the rough waters with a touch less sea sickness, why not give it a try, right?

Wishing you patience, wisdom, luck and love when you are feeling like you are beating your own dead horse.

❦ BRYN ❧

Glimpse of Light

Ways we got through each day:

- Blasting "I Miss You" by Blink 182 on the way to the hospital
- Dance parties to step music my Grandma gave us (when I was healthy enough to do so)
- Playing thousands of games of Scrabble at each meal for a distraction
- Shredding magazines when angry
- Eating on a plate that has the word "Celebrate" in big letters around the rim
- Watching my kitten pounce on my dog
- Doing tons of "I Am..." poems
- Bubble baths
- A LOT of hugs
- Cry fests and screaming matches
- Cleaning
- Looking at pictures of when Cam and I were little
- Meditating with the Oprah/Deepak 21 Day Meditation

Ways mom helped get me through the day:

- Sobriety chips - Story time: One day, on the drive home from the hospital, I said to mom pretty frustrated, "I feel like I should get a sobriety chip every time I don't throw my animal cracker on the ground or hide my food." A few days later mom told me she had a surprise for me and came into my room all smiley. She pulled out an old baby wipes plastic container and opened it up. On the top, it said 'Bryn's sobriety chips, bravery coins, and tokens' and inside were a bunch of small plastic caps with messages on them that said validations like "Good Job!", "Give Me 10!", "One Step Closer", "You've got this", "you're rocking recovery!", etc... The many plastic caps she had used belonged to tester samples of Scentsy candle wax so the container smells lovely, which is a nice bonus. I would get to pick one out after a hard meal, or even for just completing a meal without tears. I still get them occasionally—since I don't throw my food away, I feel like I'm worthy of them. I keep them all in an old coffee can that I decorated. I found art to be very therapeutic so I cut out landscape images and flowers and then did a modge-podge of images onto the can. I added words that I felt represent my recovery like heal, freedom, and growth. My can is almost full now.

- Notecards - At breakfast or lunch and sometimes in the bathroom where I get ready, I would find index cards with inspirational quotes on them. On the back would be an encouraging note relevant to how I'm feeling from mom. A couple of my favorites:
  - *"And the day came when the risk to remain a tight bud was more painful than the risk it took to blossom."* -Anaïs Nin
  - *"Even the most beautiful pottery began as a pile of mud. So, if you're a fucking mess, be like mud—at least be a fucking mess with potential."*
- Once I started back in school, the stress and triggers arose and I would try to ignore them but ended up just suppressing those feelings. Mom decided that before mealtime and right when I got home we would debrief and work through all the challenges of the school day so I didn't explode at mealtime.
- She holds me when I cry and gives me a lot of hugs even though Ed yells sometimes. This is not to say mom doesn't yell back when her patience is shot but we work through it because we're a team.

Tools to cope during the grueling recovery process

Imagine being in the deep end of a pool and not knowing how to swim. Can you visualize the flailing arms, the exhaustive battle to keep your head above water, the sheer terror on your face when you think you're going to sink to the bottom and drown? That's exactly how I've felt on more occasions than I can recount during this process of trying to get Bryn better. When there's the potential of your child dying, a little part of you dies inside. But you know that you have to find the strength for both of you, so you grasp at straws trying to find something, anything to help get you through each day (sometimes each minute on bad days). Distractions are essential to keep the focus off of the food. Through trial and error, we've come up with some "band-aids" to help with keeping one foot in front of the next during the odyssey. Some were suggestions from therapists at the EDU (eating disorder unit), some we drummed up ourselves. Here are examples of our "floating devices"—besides the given tools such as therapy—that helped us to stay afloat:

During meals:

- Scrabble

  This was our top distraction and the board resided on our kitchen table with ongoing games for months (even when the new therapy kitty, Indus would walk all over it in the middle of the night and shuffle the letters around).

- Funny YouTube cat videos or even for a while —mainly while in program— watching The Office on our phones. Any little thing that could make us smile or laugh was sought out.

- Games like *Ungame* (to help to get conversations going, sharing opinions) or the Celebrity game where you go around the table naming a celebrity or character and the next person has to find someone who's first name starts with the letter of the previous person's celebrity last name. (Example: Taylor Swift, the next person would say Simon Cowell then the next Cameron Diaz, and the next person would name David Beckham, etc...). Fun and totally preoccupies the mind with something other than the looming food.

- Soothing meditation type music or essential oil scents (room sprays). Stepping away from the table and walking around, breathing in colors (meditative breathing to calm down), talking through reasons that food is essential, etc... anything you can find to appease anxiety when it is at its highest.

- Positive affirmations after meals. Bryn must state two of her qualities after each meal. I also leave index cards daily at her place at the table with positive quotes along with an encouraging note on the back. I made "bravery chips" early on when she mentioned she felt like she should get a sobriety-type chip when she gets through meals. They are all different with words such as: "way to go", "you're doing it", "one step closer to freedom", "you soooo rock", "don't give up", "Oh yeah!!", "you are beautiful", "you're strong", etc... It's true that now, a few months in, I somewhat have lost the habit of giving those out but I have to say, they were so helpful in rewarding her for facing her fear of food several times per day.

- Putty (like silly putty) that she could play with or an anxiety stone to help alleviate the stress as she ran her fingers over the smooth, cool surface.

- Reward jar: we have a mason jar at the table with sticky notes and a pen next to it. Whenever Bryn feels good about something she has faced, she jots it down on a post-it and puts it in the jar. This focuses on the positives and is a great reminder on less hopeful days as we see the many sticky notes filling the jar up.

On days where there was anger or exercise urges or feeling blah:

- Tearing the pages out of magazines.
- Buying an old scale for cheap at Goodwill to have for the day she'd like to take a hammer to it.
- Pounding the heck out of my bed. That is one I'm particularly fond of.
- Having a dance-off: blasting the music and just going crazy dancing like there's no tomorrow. I will tell you that every time we've done that, the whole time we were jamming, we would have smiles plastered on our faces.
- Walks and/or hikes in nature. We actually found a painted rock of a tree on one of our walks with the word "patience" on it. We were utterly mind blown as we had both been tearful a few minutes earlier from frustration at the length of this arduous recovery process. I had just explained to Bryn that we were in the midst of planting the seedlings, that we'd have to be patient, allowing them to take root and giving the time needed, along with water and sunshine. With that recipe of love, they'd be sure to start to grow. It was serendipity to find that particular message at that precise moment in time. There has been a movement of painting and leaving inspirational rocks in our community so we painted our own and proceeded to leave them on trails during our walks as well. It feels good knowing we might brighten someone else's day, in return. We love healing in nature and we find it truly grounds us.
- Mindfulness and meditation. Bryn finds this difficult because, well, it is at first. It takes time and practice learning to quiet the mind and find stillness but I keep forcing it onto her because I believe it becomes a vital tool for centeredness.
- Yoga. We adore Yoga. How we feel afterward physically and mentally is outstanding.
- Books and pens: We both spend a lot of time reading along with writing. Reading is a wonderful distraction taking us into different stories (giving us a reprieve from the reality of our own lives) and writing is healing and cathartic to us.
- Reading or watching positive reminders that there's a purpose to our lives and when all else fails: Brainwashing the heck out of ourselves.

Bryn also taped up a bunch of pictures of herself from when she was a little girl onto the bathroom mirror. It helps because she would never starve that beautiful, innocent, precious child. We would also tape cut-outs from magazines to her closet doors that were motivational and declared them "reasons to live".

As you can see there are quite a few tools. I'm sure I've probably forgotten to list some and am pretty positive we are still bound to find new ones. We are adding to this huge toolbox that's helping to rebuild ourselves through this crazy, painful, yet enlightening pilgrimage towards the destination of freedom that full recovery will deliver.

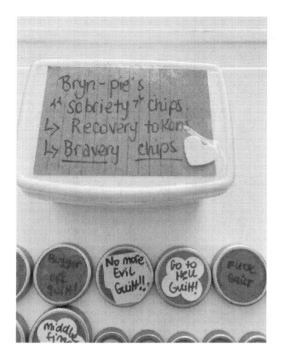

Bryn's bravery chips

❦ BRYN ❦

An explanation of my Identity

At this point, I've become a lot better at explaining my situation to people. The reason I told no one before I left was because I felt like I didn't have the words to even attempt to describe what was happening to me. I was living it and had no idea what was going on in my head or what was happening to my body. A week into Program, I finally told someone. I would say the first few people I told, I was a bit shaky because I still struggled with my words. I had all of these big emotions inside of me swirling around and I wanted to be able to explain the depth of it. I felt like I somehow had to justify myself so that they knew my illness wasn't a choice or something I could just get over with a snap of my fingers. Due to the lack of education regarding eating disorders, most people don't have an inkling about the complexity or underlying development of an ED.

Even now, after several months, I still haven't told many people because I find it quite exhausting trying to explain it all due to its stigma and intricacy. On the other hand, though, I feel it's very important to get the word out and educate as many as possible, to share what it's like from the inside world of disordered eating. It's not out of shame that I choose not to share with many people. I have worked very hard at not feeling ashamed of myself. I have nothing to feel ashamed about because I did not choose this life and I am fighting every day to stay alive and conquer my demons. Like I said in "Depression vs. No Depression", I am not my eating disorder. I'm Bryn, a human being with interests, quirks, vices, a favorite color, a personality, struggles, hopes and dreams, hobbies, and complexity. Just like anyone else. An eating disorder is only part of me, it is not all of me, it doesn't encompass all of who I am.

It can be tricky attempting to explain that perspective to others. It's one thing to try and explain simply the eating disorder part, but the anxiety, depression, and OCD tendencies are all intertwined with one another. I've learned the words to begin illustrating what living my life is like through trial and error and am confident I will, with practice, become great at explaining it.

✽ KC ✽

Our world being turned upside down

We're about six months into this life change. There are numerous ways that this eating disorder has wreaked havoc on our lives. For starters, Bryn had to take a long leave from school to be in Program while I initially took an unpaid leave from work only to end up having to resign when I realized that the road to recovery would be much longer than I had originally anticipated. While in Program, we just focused on getting through each day. It's kind of like a marathon, you're not going to look at it like: "holy crap I have a whole 30 or some miles to run", you're going to keep reminding yourself to just run one more mile, then one more. When the last day of the six and a half weeks arrived, both Bryn and I were amazed at how fast it had gone although looking back, at the beginning especially, the days felt long and frankly, I kept telling Bryn that it really was like the movie Groundhog Day. I have to remind myself of the fact that we got through that time, therefore we will get through this as well.

While she was still at the hospital, they eased her into having meals at home—first breakfast, then dinner, and then, eventually, she got weekends out. It was around the time of the end of hockey season for my son, Cameron, and I, of course, wanted to be there to support him as his team went to both league and state championship games. I would bring Bryn along but she found it to be unbearable. Her anxiety would creep up with the cheering, buzzer and any and all loud sounds. It was so surprising to me because she has been around hockey rinks for more than half of her life. Yet another element we discovered: she's always had anxiety unbeknownst to us but was initially able to manage it. First through her perfectionism then through the eating disorder. As we've combatted those two things, in essence trying to kill off both Penelope and Ed, her anxiety has had nowhere to go so it just explodes, bubbling over into every aspect of her life and she's having to learn to manage that anxiety with her newly learned skills. Since the anxiety was escalating into full-blown panic attacks, her team decided to start her on medication as she had asked for something more to add to her "toolbox". Her father and I were both very hesitant as we don't necessarily love what we've seen antidepressants do to people and I had read many years ago, an article about teens on antidepressants and suicide but we wanted to try to help her so agreed to give it a whirl. After a week, the anxiety was still omnipresent so they upped her dosage. Within days, I saw her mood decline into full depression; something she had never had before. It got really ugly with her actually voicing that she no longer wanted to live. I also walked in on her banging her head on the bathroom sink one evening, and that was it for me. I was scared shitless so we stopped the meds. After a few more rough days, Bryn began to come back, as if a veil had lifted. I was ecstatic, she was smiling and laughing again. She admitted to me that NOW she realizes the difference between being in the dumps, being "blah" and true depression. Since I always try to make sense of even the worst things, I told her that it was probably a hidden gift that she got a glimpse of that so she can better understand others who suffer from depression or suicidal thoughts. A few weeks later, however, the depression returned and she wanted to try another antidepressant. That one really helped. Now, please note that I am by no means bashing the use of antidepressant medication nor am I advocating for it. Every person is different, some people truly need it or only need it for situational depression. I am merely explaining what our own experience was.

All this to say that yes, things are most definitely challenging. Our worlds are still pretty upside down even as we are learning to adjust to our new normal. I'm still not working as I write this. Cameron is still living with his dad because he feels that everything revolves around food and often gets frustrated, yet he keeps it in because he knows Bryn is struggling. We've kept to ourselves more. Again, not out of shame but out of lack of energy to try and explain this massive life change to acquaintances or neighbors. Our neighbors have actually appeared to be completely oblivious to the fact that Bryn's car was parked outside for the longest time. We've had to try hard not to let ourselves be hurt by this. And when I do confide in some of my closest friends, there's always this shock on their part. It truly is terrifying to those who know Bryn, no one would have guessed something like this could happen to her because she has always had so much going for her and such outward confidence. I have not gone out with friends for lunch, dinner or a drink or any of the events I've been invited to. I often feel that I don't have a life outside of meal prepping and food consumption. I miss the independence that I had acquired as the kids got older and more self-sufficient. Once upon a time, I could go do something and tell the kids to fend for themselves for dinner, not that it happened often but that option used to be there, it was available to me. It no longer is... for now. I'm constantly reminding myself that this is a temporary stage. I won't have to feed Bryn until she's fifty. I also try hard to see the positives instead of dwelling on the difficulty: I tell myself that I'm lucky to be able to nourish her and that feeding her is loving her back to health.

So, when you feel defeated, please remind yourself of that as well. As parents, we've often had to use the phrase: "this too shall pass". Use it now more than ever. It will give you that extra boost of energy to hang on for just one more mile...

❦ BRYN ❧

First Exercise

A bike ride up the hill to the library: quite possibly the most innocent act one can do when they're little, some of their first displays of independence. Only, I'm not little, I'm seventeen. And this isn't a story about innocence. It's a story about anorexia and the long arduous mountain hike in attempts to reach the top of a never-ending fourteener called recovery.

As I rode my bike to the library, being one of the first forms of exercise I could do after months of staying still and being told to sit down, I was feeling pretty liberated. Less liberating, though, because Ed had a sense of control. And I knew I wasn't the one holding the reins or steering the wheel when I lashed out at my mom for imposing limits on how far or long I could ride my bike for. I can see, now, why the limits were for my benefit.

Upon further reflection, I decided that maybe it would be a good idea to abstain from exercise until I felt I was the one in control—once I no longer reacted like a junkie getting a first taste of scoring their drug of choice. I figured I could go on hikes with my mom or friends and do yoga when I felt it beneficial but I would no longer give into Ed's expectation of overexertion type workouts. Yet another attempt at striking a balance. I realize that if I'm doing it because it's enjoyable and I want to, then it's Bryn in the driver's seat and not the pesky eating disorder.

❦ K C ❦

Ed's role in exercise

I've come to realize that as soon as Bryn does any kind of activity, whether it be a hike, walk or bike ride, Ed comes in like a vampire getting his first whiff of blood, taking Bryn hostage until she becomes driven by eating disorder thoughts all over again. She gets irritable, wants to exercise even more, eat less, as if thrown back into the throes of the vicious cycle. It is hard to witness that change in her. She often voices that she just wants to be able to run or go to the gym again and is angry that her therapist and I won't allow it yet. I have to explain that she's just not there yet. The day that she wants to run, not Ed, we'll reassess.

I'm sure that by now, you're tired of me rehashing the fact that Ed is a mean bully but I don't know how else to describe it. That's the reason I nicknamed him "Dick-head Ed", I apologize right now if that's offensive but that is how I feel and I will continue to voice my feelings throughout this exhaustive quest towards Bryn's freedom from the constraints of anorexia.

*2019 Update: Bryn is a freshman in College now and walks or skateboards around campus a lot. I still have to remind her to bring snacks along with her and eat more to make up for all the walking.

**2020 Update: We are two and a half years from being released from the recovery program and Bryn is now able to admit that she loves being active but hates running and will not exercise for any other reason than it being for fun and her wellbeing. If there's even a doubt that she wants to exercise for weight loss, she reconsiders. Going into her Sophomore year of University, she wants to join hiking clubs and yoga but is equipped with the knowledge that she will likely need to take in more calories (energy) if she does that. Huge strides right there!

***2022 Update: Bryn is in tune with her body. She eats when hungry and exercise is no longer a must. She realizes that she gets plenty of exercise while walking around campus or work. One would never suspect her challenges from five years ago!

❧ BRYN ❧

The Lies

One of my most prominent values is honesty. I find that it's the foundation of so many other values: honesty breeds trust which transforms into loyalty. To me, without honesty, to oneself, to loved ones, to strangers, to surroundings, all other values lose their purpose.

Looking back, I can see all of the times I lied—or really Ed did the lying while Bryn sat back and watched. I made my brother lie for me and keep my secrets about how little I was eating. I threw away and hid meals then told my mom I ate them. When she would make me bring a smoothie juice, I'd give it away to one of my friends or dump it down the sink. I lied about working out. I lied to my friends when they went out to eat. "Oh, I already ate," I would say or I'd pull out the other excuse, "I don't think they have anything vegan there so I'll eat before." I lied about the reason I was out of school when going to doctor's appointments. If my friends knew I was at the doctor, I'd lie about why.

The guilt I would feel about lying to all the people I love was hardly a fraction of the guilt I felt when I ate. The guilt I felt for throwing perfectly good food away was nothing compared to what I felt when the food hit my belly. Ed would comfort me and caress my cheek telling me that I was lying for all the right reasons— I was protecting myself, those are the lies he ultimately fed me.

In reality, Ed thrives off of dishonesty and secrecy. I was lying to protect our love affair. I was lying to keep him close. I refuse to lie on behalf of Ed now. After I determined the difference between Ed and my values, I made a conscious decision to only live by my own values, no matter how many fits Ed threw about it.

There have been several occasions where I could have hidden food or not eaten. Snacks I had to eat at school when A. or L. couldn't be around or available to hold me accountable for eating. I had to do it for myself. Ed screams and yells until I'm on the verge of tears but the last thing I want to do is say I ate when I only ate a portion, or really when the food ended up in the trash. So I eat the food to preserve my values and the value of my well-being.

❦ KC ❧

Drowning in a trilogy of pain

I'm sure you've heard the saying "mind, body and spirit must all align". I used to cringe at that but know it to be valid in order to achieve complete harmony within your whole being. I'm hurting physically, emotionally and spiritually right now, there's that trio. I've always held emotions in my body, that is probably why I was diagnosed with Fibromyalgia at the tender age of nineteen.

The stress of fighting Ed and trying to help Bryn has had a tremendous effect on my physical well being. And in a big way. Since we are now out of the crisis zone, I'm on a mission to self-care. I've started my own therapy outside of our Ed therapy. I was finally convinced that an antidepressant could benefit me approximately ten months after we embarked on this crazy rollercoaster ride because I was basically crying every day. It had all finally caught up to me. When I'm in survival mode, I tend to just forge ahead and plow forward. But lately, I simply ran out of gas. Now, I'm walking more, partaking in yoga, getting acupuncture, Reiki, having other energy work done, working on mindfulness—which is what I call my spirituality. I'm focusing on staying in the present so that fear and anxiety can't railroad me. I'm betting on this trifecta of mental health, physical health and mindfulness to reduce the inner and outer pain.

As much as I try to stay positive and see that silver lining, I also know that some days just suck, they are plain crap and that's ok. This life-altering event beats you to the ground and it's alright to allow yourself to lay there for a bit and throw yourself a pity party. I know I do. But then, it's vital to get back up and plan the next trajectory in kicking Ed's ass all the while continuing to take care of your loved one affected by the disorder but especially yourself. Heads up, repetitiveness ahead: you've got to put your own oxygen mask on first. I may preach it often but it's because it is vital for your own sanity and self preservation.

Just like we are battling Ed, I am also battling chronic pain, emotional woes and working on challenging my thoughts when negative. Why? Because I deserve to have a well-balanced life once this is all said and done.

❧ BRYN ❧

But the doctor said so

Before Ed and I were found out, it was time for the dreaded annual doctor's visit to make sure all my body parts were in all the right places. When my doctor said I was at the perfect weight and that I could stand to lose or gain five pounds and still be in the healthy range, all Ed and I heard was that I was five pounds too heavy. To me, I wasn't at a perfect weight unless I was underweight and you could see the outline of my bones through my skin. This was still all in secret.

I set goal weights for myself, starting with the five pounds where I still would be considered healthy. But being the perfectionist that I am, I didn't just want to do that, I wanted to go above and beyond, lose as much weight as I possibly could—which looking back at it now was "as much as I could" before my mom intervened and got me help.

Of course, my doctor at the time had no idea how mean Ed was or that I even had the warning signs of an eating disorder so she wouldn't have had any inkling on how triggering that one statement was: "You're at the perfect weight; you could lose or gain five pounds and still be healthy." But I didn't want to be healthy. I wanted to be thin, beautiful, and powerful. It started with me trying to eat healthier and exercise more to see if it would make me feel better while quieting Ed's ruthless, tantalizing voice. Soon, however, the restriction just progressed into much more dangerous and limited territory.

❧ K C ❧

Bullying, Suicide, Anorexia, oh my

Over the years, schools have done an exceptional job of educating their student population about the effects of bullying and starting anti-suicide campaigns. They preach to the kids that they must speak up if they suspect such occurrences. I'm so grateful they are doing this because those topics are extremely important and they've always been near and dear to my heart. I must admit, though, I'm baffled by the fact that eating disorders are rarely, if ever, discussed. I would like to see this change because they are just as dangerous and can be deadly. If kids were taught to recognize the signs and speak up when they suspect a peer of starving themselves or making themselves vomit, it could save a life.

Bryn told me that in the seventh grade, in health class, they did briefly go over anorexia and bulimia but there wasn't enough emphasis as to the dangers of these illnesses. On the flip side, they also went over obesity (since it is such a prevalent issue in this country) discussing what healthy diets should look like and providing a calorie counter. She admitted to me just recently that it was at that time that she first started calorie counting, although back then, she couldn't fathom how someone could starve themselves and not eat or even force themselves to throw up. Health class, in essence, gave her the first tools towards restriction. I know the curriculums were not designed for that, I just wish there was more said about the devastating effects of eating disorders and would love to, one day, be able to tour schools and speak out about this issue. Bring some much needed clarity to the subject at hand.

I've often wanted to ask Bryn's friends if they suspected at all the path she was on and if so, why they didn't confront her or approach me but I don't want them to feel bad or guilty. Knowing would help me with my approach in educating others, which is a grand desire.

If we're completely transparent, the future starts with this next generation. There are too many stories of adolescents not knowing how to cope with daily pressures. They turn to teasing others, booze, drugs, self-harm, starvation or purging, sex, and sadly taking their own lives—anything and everything to seek to numb their stress. It is vital that mindfulness and proper coping skills be taught from a tender age. I wish I had started those practices with my kids sooner.

It's time that we stand up and state loud and clear that we're tired of seeing our children bullied, harming themselves or worse: killing themselves.

⚘ BRYN ⚘

Perfect Recovery

"Be perfect. Do better. Try harder. Never mess up." The sounds boom around my head in constant pangs. Penelope doesn't allow me to do anything but perfectly (which is quite impossible if you don't know this by now) so really, I never win. I feel as though my recovery has to be a smooth road, like the ones Lightning McQueen puts down in Radiator Springs— this is a Disney reference to the movie "Cars" in case you're wondering what the hell I'm talking about.

I don't allow myself any grace in the department of recovery or really anything involving me because in some way I've convinced myself that I could have done better. Due to the nature of recovery being so particularly personal and unimaginably difficult, I have to constantly remind myself that where I am is right where I should be.

My mom asks me sometimes when I'm ganging up on myself, "Well are you trying your hardest?" I typically answer, while swiping at my hot tears avoiding choking on them, with a faint sound resembling "yes" because I am truly trying. I really am giving recovery all of my might and am fighting Ed with my purest mustered-up strength. Then she smiles and answers "Then what's the problem? You're doing your best." And I am learning that my hardest and my best is enough. It's actually more than enough.

❦ KC ❧

Celebrating the victories, big or small

It has been almost a year since Bryn was admitted into Program. I have witnessed some huge feats in the last few weeks. Bryn has been eating ice cream with cookies at night. You just can't even imagine what a ginormous step (or one thousand ginormous steps) that alone has been but then today, she came home from school and made her whole lunch by herself, without me prompting. Some may think: "well, she is an eighteen-year-old adult…" and I would just dismiss that thought because those people haven't walked a single foot in our shoes. I seriously wanted to jump up and down, hooting, hollering what a proud mama I am. The feeling was similar to when she took her first steps or learned to use the potty or learned how to ride a bike for the first time. Yes, the pride that was bubbling up in my chest was that intense. It may have been the first real moment where I knew without a doubt that Ed would NOT win.

This has come at a time where anxiety was starting to build up within me as we've had a bumpy ride with maintaining Bryn's weight. The first big hurdle was the surgery for her wisdom teeth removal, she had lost five pounds in five days. Upon hearing that news, I had to bite the inside of my cheeks to keep the tears that were stinging my eyes from spilling over. It was awful but I was determined we'd regain that weight, and I successfully did just that by incorporating high-calorie smoothies and milkshakes into her meal plan. This was back in the summer, a couple of weeks before Bryn's senior year of high school commenced. Immediately following the beginning of the school year, as in the second day of school, Bryn came down with mononucleosis. Could the timing be any crappier,

I'd wondered. This was over five months ago, since then, Bryn has had so many illnesses, up/downs, viruses, mono relapses, etc… She has missed more school days so far than she has attended. We are pretty convinced that it is due to the starvation wreaking complete havoc on her immune system, nearly killing it but not quite. She keeps getting whatever cold has been going around which then turns into laryngitis. This has happened almost on a monthly basis. The last time we went to the doctor's office, I demanded tests be done because I couldn't believe she'd keep coming down with the same viruses over and over. Luckily, all the blood work came back fine, so, her immune system isn't completely shot. However, the continuous sinus drainage and recurring sickness has made her extremely nauseous so she has not been wanting to eat as much. Just yesterday, I was concerned. I was looking into the future, wondering if Bryn would be capable of forcing herself to eat when sick if I weren't around. That anxiety kept creeping in, I would shoo it away but the turmoil resided in my subconscious. I had a difficult time falling asleep, for example. That's why Bryn making her own well-balanced lunch today was a BIG deal! It helped me let out that breath I feel I have been holding for months and months. A sigh of relief. Hope. That beautiful four-letter word that keeps getting us through.

Today was a very big jump in the right direction, so I absolutely do want to pause and reflect on it. Savor this moment because Lord knows how many tough junctures we've had over the last year. This stage is right up there with the day she actually ate a granola bar without a meltdown. I had pledged, a while back already, to take notice more and comment on the smaller (but still extremely important) steps along the way. I believe in focusing on the positives, how far we've come instead of how far we still need to go, which has also really helped to take the pressure off of Bryn.

There are also tools that have aided us both when we each felt like the other was dismissing us as not being "good enough" or doing a "good enough" job. Bryn's therapist suggested we keep a notebook on the kitchen table for us to write out the other person's qualities. It's funny because when the kids were younger and fighting, I would use that same tool —making each write something that they liked about their sibling. I know that when we feel like we are drowning in a pool of cow manure, it's difficult to think of applying those tools. Again, when you choose to focus on the positives, that brutally bumpy road becomes less treacherous. It softens even the harshest blows.

PART THREE

A year and beyond

❧ K C ❧

A Huge Anniversary

A whole year has gone by since Bryn was released from Program. What a year it has been! Lately, anytime I sit quietly at my dining room table looking out at the mountains, I reflect on the past 365 days in complete amazement of what my daughter and I have endured together. I am not exaggerating when I say we've gone through hell and back. I remember the numerous times that Bryn was struggling during a snack or meal, where I'd look out those same windows feeling so trapped and alone. I would think, *There's a whole world out there and not a single soul knows the prison we are in right now.* Thankfully, those mountains brought comfort. At some point during Bryn's treatment, I had mentioned to her that this recovery was like climbing a fourteener, which is a mountain with an elevation of over fourteen hundred feet. It had long been a goal of ours to hike one together. The analogy was to show that as long as we kept our eye on the summit, we'd keep moving forward. This metaphor first came into play when she felt that she couldn't possibly consume the amount of food we were serving her. Her meal plan was increasing every day and every week as she needed to regain the lost weight but also to get back her goal weight. This was surely the climb of a lifetime… Hence the title we had come up with.

So how are we doing a year into recovery? I can say that Bryn is absolutely doing much better yet there are still some setbacks at times. Lately, she has taken full control over her food but has dropped three and a half pounds which will need to be regained. I am so proud of her taking accountability for nourishment. She also knows that I'm always completely ok with having to take back some of that responsibility for a while, if need be to give her a rest. In all seriousness, even someone without an eating disorder sometimes finds meal planning difficult at times. Who has never said: "what should we do about dinner?", not a soul I'm sure. She has had a whole lot to juggle lately: getting through senior year, applying for scholarships, working as a hostess at a restaurant, babysitting, tutoring in French, having her boyfriend so far away in the Navy, and all the other pressures teenagers feel getting through high school. I'm so very proud of her and still focus on just taking things one day at a time. One of my all-time favorite quotes is by Bil Keane: "Yesterday is history, tomorrow is a mystery, today is a gift which is why we call it the present." The mindfulness, in learning to just be by staying in this moment, that I have been practicing has completely been a blessing in surviving all of this. I try to pass it along to Bryn as well. It helps when anxiety or worry are mounting. I think that she is above most eighteen-year-olds with her knowledge.

Because things have been more challenging to balance lately, Angela suggested that Bryn do a little self-care. Bryn went to Target and treated herself to some cozy jammies and a new book. As she was being checked out, a grandmotherly woman asked Bryn how she was doing so Bryn briefly explained that since life's been chaotic she was "treating herself" and the sweet old lady responded: "well it's good that you aren't doing that with food". Bryn texted me immediately. That was absolutely the worst thing she could have heard at that moment. Obviously, the lady had no idea but the mama bear in me wanted to drive over to Target and go full preach mode on her. Then, I had to step back with the realization that we will have to deal with remarks like that, ones that rub us the wrong way and are triggering, for the rest of our lives. And we have to be like the feathers on the ducks: let the water (things people say that are triggering) slide right off our backs...

As Bryn went to visit her boyfriend where he's stationed, she decided to be spontaneous and get her first tattoo: a small wave which represents the water siding off a duck's back as a tribute to me and what I taught her, she told me that I was the inspiration for it. Such a meaningful token. The thing is, we were supposed to get our first tattoos together once she was eighteen, we had decided long ago on butterflies—since she is my butterfly. A few months back she drew the design herself and incorporated the eating disorder recovery symbol along with our initials. So, I was a bit disappointed even though we weren't completely set on that particular one. Rather than being bummed out or getting mad, I decided on impulse to surprise her with my very own first tattoo and got the Yin and Yang symbol that I've desired for a long time. It was the perfect time as my word for 2018 was balance. These tattoos have given us such a sense of empowerment. This was our unique way of marking a milestone in the recovery process. I would never imply that it's the right thing for everybody but it brought us joy. We are all individuals with different ideas. With that being said, I wanted to share what has inspired Bryn and I and how we chose to commemorate our journey thus far.

This past week was National Eating disorder week and Bryn wanted to do something for it, so on a whim, she approached the Dean and head of the National Honor Society of her High School asking to raise some awareness by putting posters up and having a bake sale with some trivia cards with facts on eating disorders. Bryn got the go-ahead and whipped it all up in a day! The money raised will go to the EDU at Children's hospital because while we were there last year, we heard some horror stories of kids being released sooner than they should have been for reasons of lapses in insurance or not having sufficient financial resources. From that moment on, we decided that we'd try to help raise money whenever we could so that they had funds to tap into instead of discharging a patient prematurely, which could result in a full-blown relapse. I firmly believe that part of Bryn's successful recovery has been due in large part to the fact that we have gone all in. There were times I had to fight, like refusing she be discharged from Children's since I couldn't find a qualified external therapist. I needed the assurance of continued specialized care for Bryn, so I called Angela, who was the one to admit Bryn, and told her I wouldn't allow Bryn to be released without follow-up care. I explained all the problems I was having, that I had made over forty calls to no avail. I couldn't find anyone with a specialty in eating disorders (something I insisted on) that was open or took our insurance. It was disheartening but by the grace of God, Angela said that she actually had an opening and was willing to take Bryn on. YES!! We've been tenacious because we needed to be. Full recovery is a battle and people should not have roadblocks like lack of insurance or money. A future goal of ours, therefore, is to have a scholarship for those in need.

I guess if I were to sum up how I feel after a year, I'd have to admit with a grin: victorious. I've been able to keep my baby alive, provide her with tools to fight for her own life, and become stronger in my own sense and appreciation of self. Yes, I'm a dreamer, a hopeless romantic and an optimist but I also have a nice grip on reality and am fully aware that we are not entirely out of the woods. We can never let our guard down because Ed wants nothing more than to bulldoze his destructive path back into our lives. I'm here to say: I'll be damned! We are stronger than that jerk!

❧ BRYN ❧

The Utah Motivator

I have motivators hung up on my closet door. They're little decorated note cards with pictures of the things I need to live for. What I eat for. Examples: Traveling (picture: a small paper airplane). Hiking (picture: the mountains with little trees freckling the triangles). Friends (picture: a curly-haired stick figure holding hands with another stick figure). Concerts, college, recovery kitten, my future, etc.

As a teenage girl who wants nothing more than to be normal and have unforgettable experiences, I've had this goal of visiting some of my friends in Utah, for a long time. The vision is that my girlfriends, A. and L., and I would all pile up in one of our cars and drive the five hundred miles to Mormon country and honestly, I know for a fact that we would have the best time ever. It's just, well, there's the issue of food. And anxiety. And depression. And being out of my routine. It seemed like such a distant and unachievable goal but if you've learned anything about me so far, I'm pretty stubborn and determined so I've decided it's going to happen. Mom hasn't exactly come to the same conclusion quite yet. The definitive decision is still in the brewing stages.

There are of course conditions. The biggest being, if I am to go, I have to eat. (The obvious.) So that I don't have to make the food decisions and overthink every menu and meal, causing anxiety—which would probably make me start crying—I would jump straight into completely normalized eating and mimic exactly what L. and A. eat. No tears!! Whenever they eat, I eat. If we have to stop at a gas station for a snack, then I partake in the gas station food road trip experience. Scary. Yikes. But it's what I want to do because I want a vacation, I want to see my friends, and I want to go on a road trip with my people. I want to live my life and I'm not going to let Ed stop me.

Of all people I know, I could rely on A. and L. to hold me accountable ensuring I get my nutrition and to help me work through the anxieties that may arise. I would also have my trusty friend Zoloft and really, I wouldn't be too far away from home, considering people my age tend to go to Cancun for spring break. Mom, *mommy-ing* me, as moms do, doesn't know how she feels about three newly eighteen-year-old girls driving eight hours alone but she trusts A. and L. with taking care of me. Maybe we just have to figure out the whole turning ourselves into three boys instead or something. We're working on that.

I feel like after being a prisoner within myself for so long, experiencing independence doesn't seem like an irrational desire. I would have this opportunity to claim control of my life and do something that is very much out of Ed and I's comfort zone, but the positives outweigh all the other worries. It's worth it to experience something different. And I'll be able to tell my grandkids this really cool story about how I kicked Ed's ass and ate gas station food with my best pals on our way to Utah.

❦ BRYN ❧

You aren't skinny enough to have an eating disorder

Ed used anything and everything against me in order to make me believe that I wasn't sick. The phrase "you aren't skinny enough to have an eating disorder" bounced around in my head constantly. No one had ever really said those exact words to me except for Ed. I once dropped the word anorexic and my mom, I believe was still in somewhat of a denial stage, said that I shouldn't label it because I'm not anorexic. Ed didn't like that very much. Did I not look good (thin) enough to have an eating disorder? Why didn't I look sick? Looking back at photos of me, my mom points out how hollow I look. Friends at school would tell me that other peers guessed why I was gone, they had assumed I struggled with an eating disorder. I guess Ed and I thought we were keeping the secret pretty well, but evidently, we weren't.

There is not a weight requirement to have an eating disorder. Some patients at my program that were at their healthy weights were actually the sickest, with feeding tubes and in need of a wheelchair due to their heart rate. The seriousness of an eating disorder has absolutely no correlation to the outside appearance of the person fighting for their life. I hear of recovery stories that involve someone saying something along the lines of your weight not giving any inclination of an eating disorder and truly it makes me cringe. I know personally, if I was in the midst of my worst with Ed and someone told me I didn't look like I had a problem with my eating, it would give me so much more drive to starve even more. It would provide Ed with so much anger-filled fuel to kill me and infest my body with sickness and distortion.

I find that there needs to be more of an education surrounding eating disorders not only in adolescents but for adults as well. I tend to believe that if people gained more of an understanding about the disorder itself, those fighting the fight could access support more easily and may not be triggered by those who would have previously commented on weight or appearance. Ed is cunning and will find any way to manipulate what others say as well as your thoughts of yourself. He will downplay the severity. He will use anything as an excuse to prove that you are happy and healthy the way you are, the skinnier you are. Example: I hadn't entirely lost my period when I was at my worst with Ed— he told me it's because I wasn't sick enough and I was hardly starving myself. If I kept getting periods, how was there any way I could be ill? I found out in the program meeting with my adolescent medicine doctor, Dr. J., that I would have lost my period if I hadn't been on birth control. Because I was using birth control to regulate my periods and soothe my cramps, my body was producing "fake periods" as Dr. J. called it. The birth control forced my body to have periods though it wouldn't have done it on its own. This, to me, was a huge eye-opener in Ed's manipulation, telling me the opposite of the truth in order to get me to do what he wants more than anything— starve. It's the same concept as my demon, Edward the Excuse Maker, I just didn't recognize who that was yet.

Don't let Ed fool you into believing you don't have an eating disorder due to your size or outward appearance. Eating disorders don't discriminate by weight, gender, or race; they take anyone who they can get their grip on. Once you admit to battling this demon, Ed, you're one huge leap closer to a happier and abuse-free life, filled with so much more hope, opportunity, and empowerment.

❧ K C ❧

Shame and guilt

These two little words can become smothering when they try to take up residence in your space. If you allow them any power, they can grow to monumental proportions. In my case, with this eating disorder, they are very closely knit, they are close first cousins.

When Bryn was first diagnosed, I was reeling. Barely going through the motions of the daily treks to the hospital, trying to absorb as much information as possible and as quickly as possible, my mission: to keep my baby alive. I didn't reach out to anyone, including my best friend who lives in another state because I simply did not have an ounce of energy to do so. I think that some believe it was out of shame but that is furthest from the truth. I can say that I haven't been ashamed, not once, about Bryn's anorexia. Because I knew from the beginning that she hadn't chosen this. It chose her. No one wakes up one day saying: "hey, I think I'm going to choose to have a mental illness and even throw starvation into the mix". And I've never been ashamed of Bryn, period. There is a lot of judgment and stigma and people can believe what they want. The simple matter of fact was that I was lost in a storm raged sea, fighting with all my might to not succumb from the numerous waves pounding at me, trying to drown me. I couldn't even formulate the words and was too exhausted to try and explain something that so few are able to comprehend. I couldn't bear the thought that I'd have to explain that it's not because she wants to be skinny, that there are so many more layers and depths to this illness. So, I remained in my lonely prison. I will state this again: not out of shame but out of total lack of energy and being incapable of explanation.

Where shame comes into play and tries to screw with me is when insecurities tend to pop up, when I second guess myself or play the "what if" game. When I wonder how I didn't realize the subtle signs sooner; when

I ask myself what I could have done that would have ensured a different outcome; when I start to blame myself. Those are the times that shame burns into my very core being, resulting in feeling so guilty that I wasn't able to prevent this monster from hijacking my daughter. The reality is that I am imperfect. As much as I've wanted to be the very best mother, and have spent years doting on my children, I am perfectly imperfect, as all human beings are. I've had my shortcomings but I can honestly say that I did the best with what I had and with what I knew. In all reality, nothing I did or didn't do caused this or, on the flip side, could have prevented this. It just is. It is also human nature to want to know why bad things happen. I don't think anyone knows the answer to that, including myself. I'd like to think that the challenges we go through, even going through hell, forges us into better, stronger versions of ourselves. That reads as so naive to even my own eyes, but hey: I've always been a dreamer, believer and hopeless romantic. What has always gotten me through in life, is that belief that nothing is in vain and that we have the ability to turn something that resembles a heap of shit, into something resembling art & beauty. Don't get me wrong, I am very much human and have plenty of my less than optimistic days. I have found, however, that it's during those "down days" that shame, guilt, and any other negative emotion tries to wriggle its way into my psyche.

As I work on combating my shame and guilt, I also try to exhort Bryn in doing the same. She obviously feels guilt over different things than me, such as food. The bottom line is that feeling ashamed and guilty is utterly non-productive. We must continue to try to win the upper hand on shame and guilt and the negative feelings they produce within ourselves. I think that the more we recognize it, practice it, the better we get at not allowing it to reside within for too long. I know we will get the hang of it because I have vowed to beat Ed and all his other little demon friends that want to destroy Bryn and in essence, our family.

❦ BRYN ❦

The Closet of Contempt

I used to love shopping and dreamt that when I became rich (because my younger and innocently naive self figured it was inevitable), of having a house with a massive walk-in closet that could contain all of my shoes and expensive designer clothes, as well as my husband's—which, let me be clear, will not be Ed.

At this moment in time, however, I'm not in the least fan of clothes or closets. I'm to the point, and have been for a few months now, of feeling unpleasantly uncomfortable in clothes. I hate that my skinny jeans are tight to my skin, breaking Ed's rule of paradoxical *loose* skinny jeans. I hate when I accidentally see the size of my t-shirts or can see the outlining shape of my figure in a reflection. I hate getting dressed and being vulnerable in my nudity in front of me, myself, and I. And don't even get me started on bikinis!

I practically live in my pajamas, and I'm not exaggerating at all. Whenever my friends come over, I'm in my soft Bugs Bunny pajama bottoms that are two sizes too big, and Hippo Campus concert t-shirt. If it's too warm for Bugs Bunny, I parade around the house in an overly loose t-shirt and spanks. I don't change into real clothes unless I have to leave the house for an appointment, in which case I throw on a sweatshirt (braless) and some high waisted jeans. I'm living the dream, only wearing PJs and instead of feeling bad about it, I look forward to getting into my most comfortable sleepwear.

Since the summer is rolling around pretty quickly (which means I can't stay in my pajamas forever, unfortunately) and I won't dare to try on my old shorts or tank tops, clothes shopping has been in order. Three days ago, my mom and I went to try on some high waisted shorts and shirts that I could feel somewhat comfortable in. Many times I asked my mom her opinion and if certain apparel made me look fat, which is what I thought I looked like. I avoided looking at the clothing sizes printed on the itchy tags and tried not to get too down on myself when certain shorts wouldn't budge higher than the middle of my thighs.

My mom told me on the way there that while shopping, I had to remember that different brands and styles of clothes have different sizings so though some things may say they're my size, they might not fit right. It doesn't mean anything about my appearance or body, it's just how the world of shopping goes.

Several articles of clothing were looked at and tried on, and a few hours later, I ended up getting only one pair of shorts and a few shirts and tank tops. And that's okay. Some of the outfits I felt okay in—even sort of cute! But with self-compassion and recognizing that Ed's lenses skew the perception you have of yourself, allow yourself to feel whatever you're feeling when clothes touch your skin.

❧ K C ❧

Letter from S

This is the letter that was written to Bryn after she visited the EDU to speak with patients and show them that there is a life outside of an eating disorder.

Bryn,

When I first saw you, I noticed a young, smiling, beautiful girl with a HUGE ray of light shining through. Hearing your experience really helped me know I'm not alone and it does get better. (over a long period of course). Even this morning I was talking with Sadie who is on staff, describing how worried I am about going home and wanting to do my behaviors at home but knowing I'd get in trouble or seeing my full body for the first time and going into my kitchen. And if I'll relapse in a year from now... Okay, I'm sure you get the point. I'm terrified of life without my ED. But after hearing your story and seeing your smile, it really touched me. Of course, right now I am still pre-contemplative but listening to your story helped me realize there is a life without ED and a life full of smiles, hanging with friends and not constantly thinking and planning your day/life around food. I really connected with how your mom and yourself would take life a second at a time. I really shouldn't dive too deep into my future worries, thoughts and wonders. I honestly have so many more questions but didn't want to annoy and flood you with questions you may find silly.

Thank you so much for sharing your story and giving me so much insight, inspiration and the hope I've been yearning for. I'm so happy I got to listen to such an amazing story and got to know more of your thoughts and how you got through them. Thank you. (underlined several times)

Sincerely, S

This just goes to show that Bryn is an inspiration to others without even knowing it. The moments like these and the pride they've brought has helped us to keep plugging away to get through the hardest parts of recovery. We both are trying to practice what we preach.

❦ K C ❦

Looking back at memories

Lately, I've noticed the memories that have been popping up on my Facebook account from two years ago, around this same period. They initially make me smile until I get flooded with the realization that Bryn was struggling, dedicating herself to starvation and I was still clueless about it. That was when she started obsessively exercising, making her vegan meals, and I just thought she was discovering her likes and trying to be healthy. I mean, what's wrong with that, right? Then my smile quickly fades, and is replaced with a sour taste.

Times like these are when I have to refuse to waste my precious energy on feelings of guilt because, quite frankly, I can't berate myself over what I didn't yet have knowledge of. Bryn is now in her freshman year of college and tells me on a regular basis that I saved her life. I'm grateful that she acknowledges the sacrifices I chose to make to get her better but I also urge her to take a lot of the credit for being brave enough to save herself. I'm all too aware that far too many stories don't end up where Ed's victim is able to go off to college two short years after plummeting into the dark abyss of their eating disorders.

We actually just learned last month that the girl I mentioned in the chapter "Ed's blemishing effects on a caregiver's psyche" succumbed to her Ed. The demons that haunted her were far too strong. She was only eighteen years old upon entering hospice. When I heard the news, I sobbed. The pain I feel for her mother—with whom I am still in touch— not just in my heart but throughout every cell in my entire body is indescribable. I will forever hail her a hero for the sacrifices she made for her baby girl. Anorexia Nervosa crept into their lives at the tender age of eleven. She stopped at nothing to find a way to finance the numerous visits to an array of recovery centers throughout the United States. She spent years going from one facility to the next, in hopes that at last her daughter would break free from the hell of restriction. Some of the stents were not six weeks long but six months.

The awareness that this outcome could have happened to my child is a direct punch to the gut. Followed shortly thereafter by a brief view of what I can only imagine to be survivor's guilt. I've come to realize that I much rather let memories come to me naturally, therefore I've chosen to abstain from social media for the time being.

❧ K C ❧

Ripple effect of educating others

I vowed very early on, well before we even embarked on the full journey of recovery, that I would educate myself as much as possible and pass on that knowledge whenever I could. Why? For starters, when I was trying to find help, I felt that door after door would close in my face as soon as I would inquire about any sort of treatment options for Bryn. I was like a dog chasing its tail. It was truly like pulling teeth trying to get answers, let alone get proper care. I was solely focused on finding the appropriate professionals before Bryn starved herself to death. All of my energy went towards that so I really didn't share with friends what was going on. Then, the fight becomes about just keeping your head above water as Program literally kicks your butt. When I was to a point of wanting to share, I would notice the sometimes unspoken words or facial expressions. It was apparent how stigmatized an eating disorder is, like most mental illnesses are, sadly. I wasn't always met with the sincere concern that my child was sick. If Bryn had any other disease non-related to mental health, there would be a flood of support or pity—not that we would want pity but you can see what I'm getting at. There was also a staggering lack of education on the subject. I actually had people ask, yes, this was several different persons, not just one individual: "is anorexia the one where they throw up?". I'll pause so that you can re-read that. We live in such a body image-focused world, I truly thought that people at least knew the essential differences between anorexia, bulimia and binge eating. It's in a sense like knowing the difference between the sun, the moon, and the stars. In the weird way my mind functions, anyway. I quickly realized that there was a huge knowledge gap out there that we need to close in order to keep the next generations educated about eating disorders. How to recognize them, steps to take to avoid developing a full-blown one if you are at risk, and in middle and high schools: knowing the importance of speaking up if you believe that someone you know is either starving themselves or purging by vomiting. They need to know the dangers associated with these behaviors, including numbers such as mortality rates. Yes, education needs to take place and I believe that we can all make a difference. It only takes one person. Then maybe another, and a ripple effect can occur.

I've always been an enormous Oprah Winfrey fan and I'll never forget when she pushed the ripple effect of the kindness movement. I would like to see something similar when it comes to mental illness as a whole: a ripple effect of kindness, tolerance, and understanding. But for one to understand, they must be taught. I'm still searching for the avenues and platforms in which to get the word out. I started with my kids' middle school because I strongly felt it was a great place to begin since in health class, in the seventh grade, they very briefly went over nutrition —including giving the kids calorie counters as methods of tracking their food intake. Followed by an overview of what eating disorders are. I met with the principal a few months back and was delighted to know that she was serious about my message and desire to tweak their curriculum. I made sure to let her know that in no way did I blame that class for Bryn developing an eating disorder. However, by giving those types of tools to an impressionable twelve or thirteen year old girl or boy who is predisposed to developing an eating disorder is a dangerous time bomb. I also mention boys because they make up 10% of patients and those are just the stats of males that we are aware of, that are diagnosed and get treatment. I agree that kids need to learn about balanced eating; now I don't even like to use labels such as *healthy* eating. I believe all foods become healthy nourishment to a body that has undergone starvation and I also avoid using the term diet. You can stress the importance of an active body without focusing on weight loss or the need for a calorie counter. I also advocated that the school put emphasis on the deadly dangers that result from prolonged starvation and/or the effects of self-induced vomiting on the body, to dive deeper into the topic so that students are fully aware. I also touched on trying to drive home the point that kids need to speak up if they feel a friend is secretly struggling with an eating disorder. It is truly no different than when we preach for them to speak up about suspected drug use, potential suicide attempts, or bullying in their peers. The meeting left me feeling victorious, honestly. The principal also offered an open door for Bryn to come speak to the kids and share her story, which I think would be such a powerful educational experience for them. For Bryn and I as well, being on this mission of desire to get the word out.

I'm still strengthening my own two wobbly legs. It is a goal to impart more cognizance because lives are at risk. Bryn and I have always said that if our message gets through to even just one person, then, it'll all be worth it.

❧ KC ❧

Another anniversary under our belts

FEBRUARY 2019

Well, we are two years out from the day Bryn was admitted into the Recovery Program. In some ways, it seems like it's been a hundred years, yet oddly, it also feels like it was just yesterday. What I can say is this: the young woman that I gave birth to nineteen years ago never ceases to amaze me. The strides she has made are bigger than I could have imagined. To mark the occasion, she got a simple tattoo with the word balance. Balancing all things in life has been something we've really tried to work on and it was meaningful to her to have it as a constant reminder. Similar to my yin and yang tattoo that represents balance in my life, it helps us to keep balancing all things a focus. I have always been the devil's advocate type. I can see both sides making it difficult to come up with the "right or wrong" of a situation at times. That's where learning to walk the tightrope and trying to balance can really come into play. Balance, like mindfulness—or anything you are trying to become more proficient at—takes time, patience and practice.

I have to say that being two years removed from the very rock bottom of this eating disorder feels at last as if the fog has lifted. I no longer fear my child's death on a daily basis. She has made tremendous progress. She's honest with me and tells me when there is stress with school, relationships, or anything else. She gives me a heads up if Ed attempts to barge his way back in. It takes a lot for her to challenge her thoughts, which in a sense is shutting him up. For that, I'm not only grateful but I find myself in awe of her perseverance, strength, and desire to explore the life that she's crafting for herself.

We find ourselves even seeing the positives of having gone through this adversity. It has opened doors and opportunities for us to hopefully be able to help. Bryn participated in a study where MRI scans were able to show the fascinating differences in the brains of adolescents affected by Anorexia Nervosa, versus teens not having the illness. We were also asked to be photographed for marketing posters to be used at various eating disorder conventions. The special part of that was that it was Bryn, myself and Angela in the photo shoot. People may have falsely believed we were hired models instead of a real patient, her mother and her therapist. Another funny thing is that Bryn's aunt, who is an eating disorder therapist, was at a convention in New York City and saw the poster. She introduced herself to Angela, who was at the booth representing Children's EDU and pointed at the picture stating: "that's my niece".

Another opportunity arose when a book was published by the Pediatric Mental Health Institute called "Sonder: Youth Mental Health Stories of Struggle and Strength" consisting of patients' stories. A fabulous way of advocating for the youth to have a voice and be heard. Bryn submitted a drawing along with her story. The drawing featured here is titled "Dancing with Death". Although it is pretty self-explanatory, these are Bryn's words describing what moved her to draw it.

Bryn's Dancing with death

I create artwork, whether it be poems or drawings, in order to express my emotions but also to help destigmatize the world of mental illness. Art has spoken to me in ways that truly make my soul feel at home. If I'm able to create something that evokes similar feelings in others, then it's significant and gratifying. The piece shown here was intended to shine a light on mental illness, specifically eating disorders. The ballerina in my piece that I chose to name "Dancing with Death" is holding a knife pointed downwards toward herself. She is also being controlled like a puppet, similarly to how an eating disorder has its hold on its victim. I, too, was dancing with death during the time I was ill—both mentally and physically. I desire to see the day where people are able to accept themselves for who they are because each body, each person is uniquely beautiful. I long to see a society that celebrates each person while learning to appreciate differences.

New life Chapter, Sophomore year of College

When Bryn was still in program during her junior year of high school, we discussed her taking a gap year before going off to university. I needed to ensure that she was strong in her recovery before even contemplating her living on her own. At the beginning of her senior year of high school, she decided she really wanted to go straight after graduation along with all of her friends and peers. She came to me with a reasonable proposition: "If I stay in the state instead of going to California, will you feel more comfortable with me not taking a gap year?". At first, I was reluctant but how could I say no to that? It eased both of our anxieties at a potential relapse knowing she was only a one-hour drive from home and more importantly from her therapist, Angela. Initially, I asked her to come home every weekend for the first month, then I'd go up there on day trips when my schedule would allow it. We talked and FaceTimed regularly as well.

A couple of months into her Freshman year of college, she'd made a new friend that, in my opinion, screamed red flags from the start. Come to find out, she also struggled with disordered eating but had never gotten help in managing it. This in turn put Bryn in a position of being her pseudo therapist. As the friendship progressed, Bryn noticed it getting more and more toxic and realized that this friend not only struggled with an eating disorder but also with drug abuse, mood disorder, and suicidal thoughts. Those things were all triggering to my daughter, especially since she was still suffering from a concussion she had endured while skateboarding during her first semester of college. She needed to focus all of her energy on keeping her own head above water. Particularly since the campus doctor had explained to her that concussions can amplify other existing conditions such as anxiety. It became harder for her to make herself eat, however, by the grace of God, she did. She's strong-willed. She is filled with a variety of passions, has a number of terrific friends, and a mother who loves her fiercely. She has built an amazing support system around herself. Trying to put distance between this friend and her had proved difficult because said friend was spiraling downhill with suicide attempts that would make Bryn feel guilty if she wasn't there for her. Luckily for Bryn, this girl had to drop out of school and go back home. I hope she's gotten the help she desperately needs as it pains me to see potential in a person that is so lost. Had Bryn been much stronger in her recovery, maybe she could have been more of a rock for this girl but I tend to say that nobody can save a person but themselves. If they don't have the desire or will to get better, you can't do it for them.

Back when I feared her going off to school, part of my anxiety was fueled by stories of relapses due to the stress that a new surrounding or big life change can cause. I had read of young adults getting to school and relapsing hard core and I couldn't stomach having to claw our way back from that hell hole again. Another big trigger for both of us that occurred her first semester was learning that one of the girls that were in the recovery with Bryn had been admitted to hospice and shortly thereafter, lost her battle to the evil disease of anorexia. My heart broke open for her mom who had spent the prior six years trying to save her daughter's life. She had sold her house, quit her job and had ventured from facility to facility throughout the country hoping that some form of treatment would take hold and work. Ultimately, her beautiful eighteen year old daughter succumbed to the demon that is Ed. I think of that every single time someone, or even Bryn, says that I saved my girl. I'll agree that I was her biggest cheerleader but Bryn is the one to have saved herself. I can't say it enough. I could not do it for her, just like my friend couldn't do it for her baby girl… I can't bring myself to even contemplate Ed stealing my daughter away from me forever. It was bad enough when he had his talons sunk deep into her. I choose to believe that his grip has finally weakened. Staying positive is how I am able to keep going.

If you've read up to this point, you've come to realize that I always search for the good in the aftermath of devastation. This experience has shaped Bryn in so many ways. She wrote some excellent essays on her experience that have awarded her many scholarships for school. If that's not a positive, I don't know what is. I myself have experienced many bumpy roads in life but I never live in regret because those hard times can mold you into becoming not only resilient but also to live in a space of gratitude for the smoother roads that lie ahead.

College has been such a great step for Bryn and she has excelled once again by making the Dean's list each semester—without stressing herself out too much and when stress was present, she used more positive coping skills such as playing the piano or writing poetry. This was all despite having a concussion her first semester. I'm grateful that she has such a zest for life with numerous interests and passions. I'm in awe of how she trudges along and can only hope that it is partly due to her seeing my resiliency when I've encountered hardships in my own life. All a parent can ever hope for is to set a good example for their children, to mirror the values you want instilled in them.

❦ BRYN ❧

A Mentorship Opportunity

Around the beginning of the Covid pandemic, Angela had recently left the Children's Hospital to start her own private practice for an eating disorder clientele. When she began putting her practice into the works, she asked if I would be willing to be a mentor for some of her patients as someone who had gone through the battle but is now thriving, happy, healthy, and living on her own as a recovered woman. Of course, I was ecstatic and more than willing to work with adolescents fighting their Eds and offered to include the option that my mentees could paint with me in my studio as a sort of make-shift art therapy mentorship. I began seeing a young girl who I will call Mentee in order to protect her identity and story.

When Mentee and I first met, we started doing sessions while going on walks so that it felt safer and more natural. I wanted to make sure that she knew I was not a scary authoritative figure, but more of a friend that could utterly relate to the hard feelings she struggled to express. She was extremely quiet and answered all of my questions with one word responses, refusing to talk about any emotions, relationships, or eating disorder behaviors. After a few sessions, I started to get pretty discouraged as we weren't making any progress and she hadn't shown any semblance of comfort talking to me. I had to remind myself that she was a lot younger with less brain development than when my eating disorder went full blown and also wasn't in a position where she wanted to get help.

I offered to paint with her but she was hesitant as she felt like she wasn't good at art and didn't like getting messy, feelings that I had felt when I was overcome by Ed. Ultimately, with her parents' involvement, she decided to meet at my studio so I could teach her how to fluid paint. I could tell she was outside of her comfort zone but she actually smiled a few times when we were together. Shortly after that progress, her mom sent me a kind email explaining that Mentee had decided to see a therapist and get more structured and intensive help than I could offer. It was a relief to know she was getting support from professionals after finally realizing that she wanted help in getting better. I hope to continue doing mentorships and art sessions with those fighting the good fight in attempts to transcend the darkness with a bit of color.

❦ K C ❧

Mother-Daughter Tattoos

Here we are, a year later than we had initially planned, January 2019, but we finally got our tattoos. At the last minute, we decided not to go with the butterfly that Bryn had designed but instead, we got each other's heartbeats from previous EKGs inked. In August I had a procedure, a spinal epidural, for pain issues. After having had some heart palpitations, they hooked me to a machine, then printed out my echocardiogram. Bryn asked if she could have it as a keepsake. I thought it was funny (and cute) that she wanted a piece of paper showing my heart rhythm. Later that fall, Bryn had fainted in class after having sustained a concussion and the hospital had put her echocardiogram in with the rest of her paperwork. That was when the idea struck me. We both adore our matching tats. I find comfort when she's away at college and can look down and trace her heartbeat with my finger and feel close to her.

I did still get my colorful butterfly that I had always wanted. Not only because I've called Bryn my butterfly since she was little, but also because my focus words for 2019 are metamorphosis, letting go, rebirth, and new beginnings. I really love that instead of a standard New Year's resolution, I choose a word that describes an action that I know I'd benefit from working on achieving (such as balance in 2018, which I still work on perfecting to this day).

Many people don't like tattoos, Bryn's father included, and I respect that. I waited until my forties to get my first tattoo and I can say that they are unbelievably liberating and meaningful to me. This was just one way for Bryn and me to celebrate our deep bond even more. I urge you to find your own meaningful way to display your profound love in a unique fashion that suits you. It can really help lift your spirits and remind you on the dark days that love always prevails. I know that sounds like such a hopeless romantic thing to say but... I'll claim it.

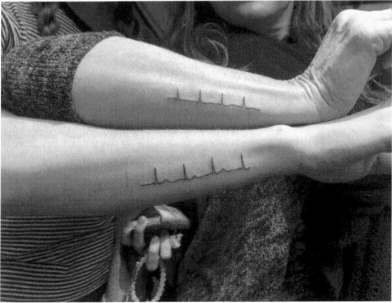

Mother daughter tattoos

❦ KC ❧

New adventures, new foods in France

Being that my entire maternal side of the family is French, I grew up in France. I had been planning to take Bryn and Cam since 2015 but there was always something that prevented the trip— including the powerful force that seized Bryn with tornado-like destruction, leveling anything in the way. The plan was therefore revised: once she was no longer in the ferocious grips of Anorexia and could actually enjoy trying various foods— cuisine being a foundation of the culture—we'd at last travel.

Our family adventure took place the summer after Bryn's freshman year of University, in July of 2019. I wanted to expose my kids to different regions of the country, the itinerary was therefore split between Paris, the south of France—The Mediterranean Sea, and Brittany—the Atlantic west coast. Although Bryn was still Vegan at the time, she didn't want to limit her experience by being so restrictive in a Country where butter is revered. She tried the various deserts and pastries made of milk, eggs and butter. She tasted the wines from the different regions as well. Sadly, she wasn't yet at a point to want to try any of the amazing cheeses since she still found cheese to taste sour, so I ate enough for both of us. This was probably the first time I truly felt that if we kept at this recovery thing, it would take hold stronger than Ed's hold had ever been.

Contemplating where we are today, I'm confident that Bryn will be able to enjoy the freedom of travel while trying all types of delicacies. She has found the enjoyment and pleasure of food again which is all I could have ever hoped for. Next time we are in France together, we will both indulge in the yummy cheese!

❧ K C ❧

Covid: the ultimate relapse test

Just as every living soul vividly remembers where they were or what they were doing upon hearing the news of planes crashing into the twin towers, the Pentagon, and a field in Pennsylvania that fateful September day in 2001, I would think the same to be true when the World Health Organization declared a global pandemic on March 11, 2020. The coronavirus outbreak shuttered schools and businesses, forcing lockdowns and social isolation. Media was raising alarm bells and many people were plunged into a panic. Mental health crises, elevation in substance use, addiction relapses have all been a result of Covid-19—forever changing the world.

Bryn's University—as most other higher education institutions in the country—decided to go entirely remote with online classes. This posed many challenges for students and professors alike. One of the things that fuels Bryn's passion for her education is in person lectures from her professors and interaction with peers. Being stuck at home, learning through a screen was demoralizing to her. Her Maymester trip to Africa wasn't able to take place resulting in yet another disappointment. She managed to get through her sophomore year by finishing it online but vowed not to return in the fall if classes were not in person.

Since she was home she had decided it would be a perfect time to potentially foster kittens. She found an agency that had three from the same litter that were being brought up from New Mexico. She jumped at the opportunity. I remember telling her that she was going to fall in love and not be able to say goodbye to them. Indeed, she was what is called a "foster-fail". Do I know my kid, or what? She ended up adopting all three of them, desperately wanting them to stay together. Caring for pets has helped her through some of the loneliest times of the pandemic. The cats have proven to be faithful emotional support companions.

When school was to commence again in the fall of 2020, Bryn decided to take a gap year. She was able to freeze her scholarships until in person learning was to resume. I supported her decision to pause her studies for a year, knowing how important being able to go to class is to her. I'm proud not only that she knew herself enough to live true to her values; but also to see her navigate a trying time such as this pandemic without relapsing has made this mama's heart soar.

❦ BRYN ❧

The Culinary Arts

As we all know, Covid was a crazy and unprecedented time. As mom said, I took a year off because I am someone that craves in-person interaction and needed the materials at school to be able to advance in my art major. The year that I took off of school, I had met a couple who had recently moved from New York City to pursue their dream of opening a private fine dining experience that offered guests a chef's tasting menu. With their culinary experience and creative imaginations, they created dishes that not only looked like a work of art but combined flavors that I could have never dreamed of.

While getting their dining experience off the ground, they needed devoted hands. They offered my roommate at the time and me jobs as the Front of House Managers which included the responsibilities of serving the guests, helping to plate the food, making floral arrangements and menus, setting up the private dining areas, and overall ensuring that the experience went smoothly for each guest.

We spent much of our time discussing food and flavors, curating a cozy yet elegant environment, and brainstorming how to entice the guests to eat with their eyes first. I gained a new excitement for food as a whole as I started trying foods that made me uncomfortable like fish and dairy as the chefs put so much thought, love, and attention into each bite. We had mutual respect for each other's art forms as mine was material and theirs, edible. There was something special watching the hours upon hours of prep work and meticulousness while cooking for their art form to be consumed by someone so appreciative of it.

They inspired me to look at meals as a work of art and as the kindest nutrition for the body. Although my employment with them only lasted about 6 months, it forever changed my view on the culinary arts, encouraging me to see food as a way to combine communities and celebrate the effort put into its creation.

Permission to obliterate perfectionism granted

"Perfectionism is a mean, frozen form of idealism, while messes are the artist's true friend"
~Anne Lamott

Reflecting back on my own personality quirks, I would be remiss if I didn't make mention of my own propensity towards perfectionism—that, at times, bordered on obsessive compulsive tendencies. While the kids were growing up, I kept an immaculate house. I felt that a clean house along with good home cooked meals was of utmost importance and I was guilty of liking things just right. I'm pleased to report that I have become much more laid back over the years and the time of being able to practically eat off of my kitchen floor is far in the past. Yet, I wonder if some of the perfectionism I displayed rubbed off onto Bryn. Children mirror your behaviors and I prided myself in illustrating to them that as E.L. James once said: *if a job is worth doing, it is worth doing well.* I believed that to be a virtuous life lesson, and it probably is. There again lies that fine line of striking the right balance. Nowadays, I'm much more of the school of thought that done is better than perfect.

I found this quote from Anne Lamott to be relevant as Bryn has been not only studying art at University, but has also been making and selling pieces on a regular basis. Needless to say, the creative nature of art leaves no room for complete order and cleanliness. When I go visit her and see dribbles of paint throughout her apartment, I smile in appreciation that she doesn't feel the anxious pull to get it up immediately. She has finally gotten to a point where she doesn't give a fuck, allowing her joy for producing art to be greater than any kind of perfectionism or anxiety about making messes. I will admit that I used to nag her about potentially losing her deposit but abstain now because she is an adult and fully aware of her responsibilities. I'm happy that she throws herself into art without abandon because, like the quote states, messes are the artist's true friend— reminding me of when she was little and I'd let her go crazy with any and all craft outlets. As a toddler I'd let her get paint or glitter all over, never stifling her creativity. So to see her get back to that childlike wonder has made my heart sing.

Bryn and I have both consciously chosen to say goodbye to Penelope and all of her painful expectations of perfection. Just as Anne Wilson Schaef stated with such eloquence: *"Perfectionism is self abuse of the highest order"*. We've decided to obliterate perfectionism. Care to join us?

Little Bryn making art at a young age already

❧ BRYN ❧

Art as Therapy

While I was in program, I looked forward to Fridays because that's when we got to do art therapy. Oftentimes I couldn't adequately express how big and strong and dark my emotions were inside me so it was nice when I could try to express them on paper or through random mediums like paper mache and collages with old magazines. Doing anything with my hands that could put my emotions into a tangible and visible form made the emotions seem a little less in control of me— like I could understand them as outside of me rather than identify within them. For a while, I was drowning in this mindset of disliking myself, not wanting to try anything new partly due to the fear of embarrassing myself or not being good at it. I essentially did not want to be perceived by myself, or the world for that matter, in a negative light. I had a hard time even just starting to paint. I had this knowing that I would disappoint myself so rather than being bad at something, I just wouldn't do it. This was a cycle I was stuck in for a couple of years before hearing that even if you create bad art, you are still creating. You are making something with your hands that didn't exist before. So yeah, maybe the art isn't great, but you learned something from it. You made it, and bad art is still art! This was amongst the most encouraging ideas I had heard regarding pursuing my passion with confidence rather than fear. Art is all subjective and most of the time it is not created for the purpose of optical appeal, it's created for the purpose of creation or for the purpose of alluding to a larger metaphorical meaning. I would urge you not to allow the self-doubting voices in your head to dissuade you from making something, anything! Creativity is essential in any healing process, regardless of how creativity is generated in the real world.

I began doing abstract painting which led me to experiment with fluid art and contemporary pour painting. Not only did this ultra messy medium challenge my OCD-type thoughts—because I would get paint all over myself, the canvas, my clothes, the table, really everywhere—but I was actually proud of my mess because it was instrumental in creating a beautiful and finished work of art. I delved headfirst into teaching myself all the ins and outs of combining chemicals with paint to achieve different patterns. I became obsessed with color, material, and technique—so much so that there wasn't much room left in my mind for Ed to weasel his way in. I taught myself how to work with epoxy resin to make three-dimensional functional objects such as cutting boards, trays, wall hangings, and shot glasses as well as decorative pieces that combine elements to yield psychedelic patterns mimicking the natural world and the patterns found in it. If we think of eating disorders as an outlet for anxiety, depression, or feeling out of control—as a coping mechanism to deal with other unmanageable emotions—I began to replace my outlet of Ed with art. Art became the activity and mindset that allowed me to escape the discomfort and overwhelm of being a complex human.

The first semester I went back to University, after taking a year off during the pandemic, I enrolled myself in two ceramics classes: hand-building and wheel throwing. I had never touched clay before that so, of course, there were some nerves that came with trying something new, especially surrounded by others that were much more experienced in this medium. I had to release all concepts about comparison and simply focus on my own personal growth through the class. Luckily, the ceramics department at CU Boulder—including all the students involved in the program—is incredibly supportive of individual endeavors as well as independent progress. Everyone is kind, joyful, and offers wonderful perspectives on the philosophy behind creation.

When I first started working with clay, I noticed something really unique: the touches you make with your hands on the clay directly correlate to the mood you're in when sculpting or throwing. I found that when I was having a rougher day, my pieces looked less lively and almost sadder. Then, on the contrary, when I am in a great mood and working with clay, I visibly see the precision of love and amusement it was created with. Many art forms are so emotionally tuned in that they are affected by the artist's mood. Yet, I have grown to love the way clay imprints emotion.

I immediately fell in love with how I needed to work with my body while making ceramics and started sculpting every day in my free time. Outside of class assignments, there were many functional and sculptural objects I wanted to bring into existence from a mound of mud so I started practicing and teaching myself the techniques in achieving the results I desired. It became a little game with myself of how difficult of a piece I could create. Sometimes based on my assignments and sometimes based on my own imagination or other artists' inspiration. Within one semester, I declared my studio emphasis to be ceramics for my art major and I spend much of my free time practicing. The amount of pieces that I've made but have broken or look nothing like how they were supposed to— or were made improperly and exploded in the kiln— are plentiful. This has taught me that the finished product is not the focus, but the act of making is.

I would like to end on this quote that spoke to me in a time where I felt a lack of confidence in my own art practice:

"I'm an artist and when you buy from me you are buying 100s of hours of failures & experiments, you are buying a piece of my heart — of my life."
-Peter Dragon

Adult Bryn doing art

❦ KC ❧

Encountering strangers clearly acutely ill from Anorexia

Every so often I come across someone who is grossly underweight, showing the numerable classic tell-tell signs of a struggle with Anorexia. Their gaunt, paper-thin-translucent-like, yellow-gray skin. Their hollow cheeks. Their sunken eyes. Their layers upon layers of baggy clothes. These sights never cease to set off my inner emotional responses. Reactions that I've worked diligently at taming and then burying in hopes that out-of-sight-out-of-mind would be just the remedy needed for keeping the denial blinders on. Before long, I'm found in a tailspin as I'm propelled down memory lane.

I find myself back at Children's hospital witnessing the new patients being admitted in conditions that still haunt me. Some had been wasting away for so long that they were bound to feeding tubes and wheelchairs. As strong as the urge to look away was, I'd find enough courage to look them in the eye and smile wanting to offer comfort, love, kindness and non-judgement. Glancing at the clarity of the blue-green labyrinth of veins protruding from their pale skin would push me over the edge. I'd end up having to look away, eyes burning with sadness and pity but also burning from shame for silently thanking the stars that my daughter wasn't yet on death's doorstep.

When I'm out and about and meet people I suspect of struggling, I do the same as I did back at the hospital. I offer kindness in any way I can: a smile, a kind word, positive conversation—all while praying that they can find the energy to break free from their self-flagellating prison. Yet, every single time, I walk away with a rock wedged in the pit of my stomach wishing there was more I could do.

My biggest hope for the future generations to follow, is a world of awareness surrounding (and compassion towards) sufferers of mental illness. Perhaps the simplicity of a mere smile isn't quite enough, but it sure is a good start, don't you think?

⚶ KC ⚶

Sia's song "Breathe Me"

Music has always been woven into the threads of my life. On my Pandora or YouTube accounts, I have several different channels waiting to be played depending on my mood. I'll admit that most of the time I like to listen to soothing melodies that have oftentimes been called depressing or melancholic. To me they are simply beautiful. I have this Sia song *"Breathe me"* saved to my *sad* soundtrack, and it tends to pop up when I'm soaking in the bathtub. I don't have enough digits to count the amount of times Bryn would either come rushing in to turn the song off or yell for me to please change it. I've asked repeatedly why she hated it so much, always getting the short answer of: "It reminds me of being in program." and leaving it at that. I could tell there was no room for prying so didn't press the issue. To this day she can not listen to that song and I'm beginning to finally understand.

The fellow mother friend from recovery who lost her daughter a couple of years back now just shared with me that her son—who was the older brother by two years—earned a full scholarship for post-graduate studies thanks in part to an essay of poems he wrote in memory of his sister. I was honored that she shared them with me—despite being broken wide open upon reading them— in view of the fact that they were exquisite. His eloquence, sentiment, and talent were full of beauty. Each piece crafted from great pathos creating a moving body of work. He also sprinkled in some of his sister's past artwork, which was equally skillful. Many of her drawings were full of shadows, revealing her inner battle. For example, she had a drawing of a girl covering her face with her hands, the words "don't listen to it" surrounding her. There was another rather sorrowful one with some of the lyrics from *"Breathe me"* swirling around the shattered girl. That's when it hit me. The song speaks of profound depression, sadness, loneliness, and longing to be helped and protected from one's own self. It is a cry for help, a desire for survival and an aspiration to stop self inflicting pain—it is about desperately wanting to be good enough to be loved. This realization sent me reeling. So, I did what I do best: I googled it. I wanted to know more about the song and was jarred to find out that the singer admitted in 2018—14 years after releasing it—that she nearly succeeded in taking her own life the very same night she wrote that song. This tidbit of information absolutely demolished me. I have still never asked Bryn if she knew any of the background of the song. Perhaps one day it will be playing on the radio in the car and she, for once, won't feel the need to change it; then I can maybe broach the subject. Although she is quite strong in her recovery at twenty one, I don't feel it necessary to bring up something that for years was a trigger.

<u>Lyrics:</u>

Help, I have done it again
I have been here many times before
Hurt myself again today
And, the worst part is there's no-one else to blame
Be my friend, hold me
Wrap me up, enfold me
I am small and needy
Warm me up and breathe me
Ouch I have lost myself again
Lost myself and I am nowhere to be found
Yeah I think that I might break
Lost myself again and I feel unsafe
Be my friend, hold me
Wrap me up, enfold me
I am small and needy
Warm me up and breathe me
Be my friend, hold me
Wrap me up, enfold me
I am small and needy
Warm me up and breathe me

My Poetry Book

During the time when I was in the depths of my struggles, I began writing poetry as a way to get my feelings onto paper. The topics of each poem ranged from being in love—since I had just fallen for someone— to living with Ed in my head, or how my family felt, and of course the journey of healing. I had spent most of the year of 2017 and the beginning of 2018 writing individual poems for my own cathartic needs.

When I moved into the dorms in Boulder, I stopped writing poems to focus on school assignments and to live in the moment. I then realized I had quite a few. Over 200 poems that could be organized into a poetry book. I named the book *4am Consciousness* and created the cover out of my own art. The book, I intentionally formatted to have three parts titled: nightmares, reality, and daydreams. The poems go through the progression of dark to light as I felt like that represents many of life's hardships that are overcome.

Just recently I realized I hadn't looked at my poetry book since I finished it in early 2019. I read the first poem that opened the book as well as the last when it hit me: You can see the utter progression and happiness that blossomed throughout the trauma.

The first poem:

> *they explain to me what happiness is*
> *i do not believe them*
> *a light at the end of the tunnel*
> *it is hollow*
> *nonexistent because the*

train is coming
it's coming.
Run.

And the last poem:

she's the girl who claps her own tunes at concerts
and checks her own pulse to make sure she is still alive

And alive, I am.

❦ KC ❧

Mother daughter tattoos part 2

Getting tattoos together as a way of celebrating certain milestones and bonding over life's meaningful treasures has become a tradition between Bryn and I now. When we had gotten each other's heartbeats done, the original plan was for us to get butterflies. I did get mine that same day and then Bryn ended up getting her butterfly a year or so later. They are very different as Bryn enjoys straight, symmetrical lines void of color for its simplicity and I like colorful tattoos with dimensional shading. I adore the fact that they are different in appearance but that the significance behind them is one and the same. We knew long ago already that our next shared tattoo would be to represent my son, Cameron, whom I've called my bumblebee. Again, distinct in design yet we both chose to position our bee right below our butterfly. This has brought on a whole new level of connectedness that we are longing to have Cam participate in as he has yet to get inked. Regardless of whether or not he ever gets a tattoo of his own, he knows that his mother and sister have an artistic representation of him on their bodies.

The relevance of these tattoos and anorexia? Valid point to ponder. I suppose the best explanation is that sharing in the experience of getting tattooed together is in part a way of celebrating the life that Ed wasn't able to take, albeit his herculean attempts to. It's our way of acknowledging that we went through a dark, scary, and tough-as-shit time but our family is here and stronger than ever. Bryn, Cameron and I have coined ourselves the three musketeers for over a decade now (that's even our group text name) and this was a way for us to honor our love.

Our bumblebee tats in honor of Cam

❦ K C ❧

The Rocky Mountainous terrain of life

"You've been assigned this mountain so that you can show others how it can be moved"
~ Mel Robbins

I tend to use analogies like crazy—so much so that it's quite possibly ingrained in my DNA. Because of my deep love of nature, those are the metaphors that flow freely out of me. The uphill battle (mountains), not drowning and staying afloat (ocean), going with the flow and not swimming upstream (river), things will turn around as storms pass (it can't rain forever), etc...

This journey with Bryn and the fact that I live with a view of the Rocky Mountains and am blessed to take them in on a daily basis has me identifying with Mountains the most; despite being an astrological water sign and loving and missing the ocean terribly.

Recovery, in my opinion, is similar to hiking in the mountains. You have to be vigilant not to lose your footing. You might have hiked that same path many times over, yet outside circumstances like rain, wind, or wildlife can change the trajectory in an instant. If you lose sight of the fact that not everything is within your control and become too cocky in attempting your climb, you could get yourself into serious trouble. Letting your guard down with any kind of recovery could mean a slide down and even a plunge off the cliff.

I would like to think that we have finally reached the summit of that fourteener we've been ascending the last several years, but that doesn't mean we can claim complete victory by not continuing to acknowledge that Ed may lurk for sometime. Is the work as grueling as it was in the beginning? No. Thank the heavens! However, we must remain aware. A lesson I liked to teach my kids was that you don't want to live out of fear but you must know the potential dangers and be vigilant. We are at a place where we can take a rest and breathe in the amazing view; look down and see how far we've come while relishing the fact that the most painful part is now behind us. Not only did we ascend that rather large mountain but we've also moved it. And *that* is an empowering feeling.

I hope you're able to keep that summit in view always. Even during times where you feel you'll never reach the top. If you keep taking one step after another, I assure you, you'll get there as well!

☙ K C ❧

Journal entry 1/27/22

Excitement! Bryn and I are in our last push of wrapping up our book that has been nearly five years in the making. Shortly after I had the self-publishing agreement in September 2019, she asked if we could put the project on hold. She needed to pause because she didn't feel ready. She had several valid reasons, school being at the top of the list. Of course not wanting to put pressure on her, I obliged. As months turned into years, it was getting more difficult to remain patient. I wasn't sure if the project would see the light of day. I figured I could continue on my own writing but soon realized it was still too raw and difficult to revisit those times.

Every two or three months I would touch base to see where she was at with potentially wanting to finish as I knew that the sooner we birthed it into the world, the sooner we could possibly help others. Without nagging I would simply remind her of all the reasons we embarked on the writing to begin with. Being adept at reading her position especially when the response was: "I'm not ready.", I would back off again. Yesterday we had a wonderful brainstorming session via FaceTime and I was thrilled to see her eagerness. I told her that all she really needed to do was a brief recap of where she is at now. I know I've written a bit more in our latest part three but it's because she's also working and going to school. As we delved into things more she couldn't wait. She kept finding more things that she wanted and needed to say. When she told me she can say with confidence that she is recovered and that Ed has zero leverage over her anymore, I teared up. Such music to my ears!

KC

It's a wrap!

Yesterday we celebrated Bryn's five years of recovery. We celebrated it with delicious food. Yep, please do read that again! It's so exciting to see her thriving. Sappy, sentimental, bleeding heart, hopeless romantic— all words that have been used to describe me. I'll own it. It is one thousand percent true that I firmly believe in the mightiness of love. I think that love breaks down boundaries and is powerful enough to heal and to transcend horrific life events. Love is a huge part of this recovery work of art that we're at last able to share.

There are still moments when I think back of our days at the hospital with a lump in my throat. It's as if the smell of disinfectant wafting through the corridors, or the blinding ugly hues of the florescent lighting, or even the loud ding of the elevator doors are forever singed in my memory. Yet, I've also chosen to never forget the security guard who greeted us with cheerful warmth, by name, as we signed in each morning. Bryn and I will fondly remember how his presence was a light in our bleak time.

I'm also proud to share that we're back to watching funny cat videos. But now it's for the pure pleasure of laughter, and no longer merely for distraction purposes. It may sound silly but I see that as another fabulous milestone.

Recently I finished a series on T.V. about drug addiction called *Dopesick*. To witness the similarities between a person run by their substance dependence and one who's addiction had become starvation shook me. The way in which a personality can transform right before your very eyes is such a powerless feeling. How addiction takes them hostage because they are at a point in life where they just don't want to feel a single thing anymore. Their addiction is better than the torment they feel in everyday life. The gut wrenching part is when you desperately attempt to share your fear of losing them and realize they're already too far gone to grasp reality. The gratitude that consumes me over Bryn waking up to choose life over her addiction to Ed may never be translated into strong enough words. To go from watching this dominant force seize her with hurricane ferocity and blow her about like lonely roof shingles in the wind, to having the honor of watching her conquer the demons and prevail is a beautiful thing.

The very last scene in *Dopesick* is a quote I'd like to share from actor Michael Keaton as I find it to be in perfect line with the acceptance that there is pain, suffering and discomfort in life. Feelings most certainly ebb and flow, if you can wait out the uncomfortable emotions, you allow time for joy to return. (Spoiler alert if you haven't seen this show yet).

"Addiction does the opposite of connecting people. It tears apart. Tears apart friendships, marriages, family and even a whole community. Part of the reason we relapse is because of pain. There's some kind of pain in a lot of us—or all of us—we just don't want to feel anymore. The further we fall into addiction, the pain says to us: 'Hell, we'd be better off just feeling nothing at all.' So we go numb, our souls go numb. Now we have a real problem. You know, pain is just pain. Not good. Not bad. Just part of being a human being. And sometimes good can come of pain. If we're brave enough, willing to go a little deeper, work our way through it, and try to overcome it; well, we might just find our better selves."

The more I practice mindfulness, the more I realize that suffering is part of life. No one is spared from it. Whether we realize it or not, or are too young to realize, or have never been taught—we have a choice as to how to ease the pain and suffering. We can use tools such as creation and art, meditation, journaling, therapy, bonding with nature, or whatever positive instrument of your choosing. My biggest wish for anyone tormented by despair is for the discovery of a passion to aid in fighting through the affliction. As humans, we are all a work in progress. I've decided to *kintsugi* myself by filling my many cracked pieces with golden light and love. I desire the same for all who've been bruised, battered and broken at times.

BRYN

The last word

It has been about three or four years now since I emotionally and physically revisited this book. Many of the passages you've read were written by me when I was 17 or 18; I'm writing to you now as a 22-year-old woman that loves life!

After going off to college, I was working so hard to live presently. I was also learning to discuss my struggles with those close to me, and ultimately feed myself for every meal and snack. I was finally in a place where I was so happy that I didn't want to do anything to jeopardize that joy. Therefore, I put our book on the back burner because rereading the chapters where I was evidently the saddest I had ever been and so hateful towards myself put me back in that mindset and ripped my entire heart open again.

In these last three to four years, I have grown and blossomed into a truer version of myself than any of you wonderful readers have gotten a glimpse of. Going to college has taught me how to independently care for myself, how to adapt to a new location and routine, how to set boundaries for myself, and love me first. I've had to learn how to "adult" with dealing with finances and work-life balance and apartment issues without panicking or coping through Ed. I've developed some incredible coping mechanisms through artistic outlets. I was also fortunate in meeting my dearest and best friend who I will call Lucia. She has supported me with unconditional love and although she couldn't personally understand the difficulty of living with an eating disorder, she chose to educate herself and ask questions in order to properly love me through it. She would gently tell me how she noticed that I would cyclically eat the same meals every day because it was comfortable. I would therefore try to push myself to eat something different or outside of Ed's comfort; Lucia and I would subsequently celebrate together.

During freshman year, I flew off my skateboard and severely concussed myself which not only messed with my memory, but my anxiety, depression, and Ed thoughts became much more amplified which was quite frustrating considering I had been doing the best that I had in a while. The doctor told me that when the brain is injured, many pre-existing conditions worsen simply because the brain is using all its energy to heal. Although that timeframe was a slight blur for me I remember leaning on Lucia along with my past successful coping mechanisms to overcome the temptation of slipping back into bad habits. Ultimately, we succeeded.

While I was concussed, another friend started slipping into deep Ed thoughts and actions as well as suicidal ideation. It was scary and after attempting to set my boundaries with her by explaining that I could not discuss certain topics like calories, weight, or overall appearance when Ed was in control. Sadly, those boundaries were not respected because her Ed was all-encompassing in every aspect of her life at that point.

After talking with Angela, Lucia, and my mom, I decided to write her a letter explaining that I wished her nothing but the best, however I could no longer be beside her in her journey to recovery because it was inhibiting my own journey to health. Writing this letter brought up a lot of feelings of guilt for me because I loved her and wanted to be able to show her love and support, but I couldn't do that at the jeopardy of my own mental health. She ended up having to go back home to get the help she needed. I received a text from her about a year after she had left saying that she was extremely happy, healthy, and apologetic for hurting me unintentionally. It was beautiful to see her transformation from being stuck in her mind alone with Ed into a joyful and flourishing woman.

I met three other amazing girls in what would have been my academic senior year of college but since I took a year off it's all a little funky, essentially it's like being a year behind. Our group of four, which we call our squadron, came into my life with an immense force of love. My girls have also struggled with eating disorders and Ed-type tendencies for different reasons. Unlike my friend freshman year who I previously mentioned, these ladies and I do not discuss triggering topics. It's more about how we can support ourselves and one another in the most healing way. Of course, this journey has been a long one, but I can confidently say that I truly love who I am, what I look like, and more importantly the kindness and acceptance I radiate. Not to forget the easy yet fulfilling interactions I have with strangers. Simply put, I love the light that I provide to this world. I'm enamored with my hobbies, my future successes and the way I've chosen to filter out people by only keeping the brightest of lights in my life.

My dad and I have a great relationship now after a bumpy few years. When I was really sick and in the deep dark depths of program and therapy, he wanted to be there for me and support me but I was so broken that I could not heal while still trying to be this perfect person I felt like I had to be so that I was "good enough" for him. After discussing these differences and hardships we had, I've come to realize that he never expected me to be perfect but he saw such potential in me that he wanted to push me in the direction of success that he defined as the right choice. Now, he recognizes my dreams of being an artist and helping others through art therapy. He has a lot of pride in me for going in the direction of my heart with fierce vigor. He fully respects who I am even though he disagrees with some of my choices such as tattoos, body piercings, and smoking medicinal marijuana. It took me being brave enough and self-confident enough to correct his comments when I felt they were out of line or could have been phrased differently.

I started teaching him the ways I felt appreciated, loved, and respected as an individual human—not just his daughter. I felt that I needed him to know that outside of being his little girl, I wanted to be recognized as a person who was not perfect but that was growing. I needed him to understand that someone trying to control my decisions was really off putting to me because in my mind it meant he couldn't trust my judgment or goals. When he talks about topics that I would prefer to table, I express gently that I don't feel that this topic is necessary at the moment and suggest that we chat about something directly important to both of us. We have grown so much as individuals and as father and daughter. February 6, 2022 which was yesterday, marks my five year recovery anniversary. It was five years ago thats I was admitted to the EDU. Dad called me while at work and left me a voicemail that brought the happiest tears to my eyes. This is what it said:

"Hey Bryn, it's your dad. I was talking to your mom the other day when she was over getting some stuff. She said you were having a bit of a celebration so I thought I'd give you a call and just tell you that you're just a remarkable person and I'm super proud of you. You're a survivor. And you deserve all the accolades you get for battling in a pretty deadly war. Anyways, enjoy your little celebration.

I'm so proud you're my kid. I wish I could see you more but I understand how that goes. Give me a call sometime, I'll be around most of the weekend. See ya."

Even reading that voicemail now fills my heart with so much happiness. It's difficult to put into words considering the heaviness of the battle but also the flip-side, which is the love I've learned because of it.

When I turned eighteen living in Colorado, I started doing research about the effects of medical marijuana and listened to other people's opinions and experiences with it. I visited with a doctor who decided I was a good candidate for using it medicinally to help with my appetite, extreme anxious/OCD thoughts inhibiting my livelihood, as well as a minor birth defect that causes my brain to slightly protrude down into my spinal column. I would like to preface that again, this is just my story and I am not encouraging or discouraging you to use medicinal marijuana but felt it would be dishonest if I did not include it in this story about our experience fighting Ed.

Whenever I used cannabis and then ate, the food tasted good for the first time in over a year. The guilt of just eating had taken away the pleasure of taste for so long. I felt as though my brain opened up in a way where I could see different truths and perspectives about myself and the reality that eating is a form of self-care and love towards myself. I saw food as less threatening and more exciting. My anxiety became more manageable and I stopped being so OCD about dirt, hairs, numbers and the need for control in every situation. I gained a new zest for nature, life, and this hippie sort of philosophy of respecting and being grateful for every living thing surrounding me, including myself. For the last four years, I have continued to use cannabis as a tool but not a crutch and it is something I often check in with Angela about just to maintain self-awareness so I don't fall into a hole of using substances as an outlet rather than healthy coping mechanisms. We have discussed ways that I can relax and recharge outside of Ed, marijuana, panic attacks, etc. I am brutally honest with myself to ensure that I never fall back into unhealthy habits and I consistently check in with my mom and my support system to keep an open dialogue about behaviors and mental health.

I was vegan for three and a half years after being discharged from the Eating Disorder Unit but I/Ed had fully convinced myself that I was not vegan as an eating disorder tendency, rather for ethics. I started being a lot looser with the restrictions of what being vegan meant and if I wanted to eat a cookie that had butter, eggs, and milk, I would! It took me another two years before I decided to fully stop being vegan and switch to vegetarian.

About six months ago, I decided to reintroduce cheese and butter into my diet in order to limit myself less because I was sick of eating the same foods. I tried mac n cheese for the first time in five years and it was practically orgasmic. Of course, when I first made the switch, some Ed thoughts popped into my head about the labels of healthy versus unhealthy but I just had to remind myself that health is equivalent to balance. Luckily my left arm tattoo says that very word, therefore, I never forget. Regardless of the type of food, it is still nutritious. Months after opening the door to more foods, I was able to celebrate my five years with a nice lunch at the restaurant where I work and made sure to get extra cheese with my meal.

When people used to tell me and Ed—when we co-existed in my head together—that the loud voices would subside and I would eventually be able to live my life without the all-consuming thoughts about food, hating myself, what my body looked like, etc., I had no doubt in my mind that they were lying. I can say now that I am recoverED, capital E D baby! The thoughts that sometimes come up when I look at myself naked or am not particularly hungry but know I need to nourish myself are so minuscule that I can easily thought-challenge, not give energy to the thought, talk it out real quick with myself or someone around me, or do something I love.

The thoughts hold no weight. Weight is only real when you give it power or assign a positive or negative meaning to it. So my thoughts hold no weight and neither does the number on the scale. I remind myself of all the things that I love about myself outside of the appearance of the vehicle that transports my soul. Outside of the nutrients I consume to continue living. Outside of all the mental illnesses that will always be with me but don't overpower me.

Those voices did not just become quieter, rather, my voice became stronger and louder.

ACKNOWLEDGMENTS

There are so many people that I'd like to extend my most sincere gratitude to, not just in the making of this book but also those who were a great source of strength and support along the way. First, I have to thank my beautiful daughter, Bryn, for showing me what true grit is in the face of adversity. Bryn, you have shown me what drive, tenacity, strength and bravery look like. I'm proud of all that you are and all that you continue to strive to be. Thank you, from the bottom of my heart, for trusting me with your life, back when you didn't trust a single thing except for what Ed was *feeding* you. (Pun intended).

To my son, Cameron for trying to put himself on the *back-burner* so I could tend to his sister. Thank you for trying to do your part during an extremely difficult time for our family. Your compassionate heart makes me beam.

It took a team of people to help keep us from drowning and without the Children's Hospital staff at Anschutz Medical Campus, I'm not sure we would have had as successful of an outcome. We had our favorite nurse, Sadie who was such a ray of sunshine. Bryn's therapist, Angela Ward, LCSW, who continues to be a true angel. We're touched that you were willing to read our manuscript in advance of publication. You have helped us to grow tremendously, thank you seems pretty insufficient. My own therapist that I only started seeing a few months into embarking on Bryn's recovery, Amanda Chaney, LCSW, has saved my sanity on more than one occasion. You taught me to give myself grace during times where I was my harshest critic in the realm of being a "good enough" mother. Our dear Wendy Strait, both Bryn's and Cam's high school guidance counselor, who has always had our backs. Thank you for always being a rock to us! To my Reiki Practitioner and friend, Rev. Erica Danielle, Soul Shift Energetics for helping Bryn and I to expand beyond our comfort zones in the name of growth. You have a true gift and I feel blessed to have been the recipient of it for the last several years.

I have also had a team of healers who have exhaustively worked to help me combat persistent physical pain. Thank you!

Of course I couldn't leave out all our friends, family, teachers, coaches, neighbors, acquaintances (too numerous to list each of you, but you know who you are!) for holding space in your hearts for us and offering prayers, encouragement and kindness. It kept us afloat. Drea Estep, my friend and sister, for believing in me and being one of my biggest cheerleaders. You helped me greatly in the editing process but your confidence in me has meant more than I can express. To my former husband for being instrumental in creating our amazing kids.

Lastly, in the spirit of gratitude, since that has been a big driving force for me to keep putting one foot in front of the other in times where I didn't think I could; I'd like to acknowledge Ed for teaching us that we are stronger than his lies. Through defeating Ed, we've courageously unveiled the mask of vulnerability.

The amount of people that come to mind when thinking of who helped me grow through such an intensely hard chapter of my life is infinite. I would like to acknowledge the many people who were prevalent in the beginning parts of my journey and are no longer — I would like to give thanks for the lessons they taught me, the growth they provided me with, and the understanding of what compatibility looks like. More importantly, they led me into the arms of my current support team which allowed me to appreciate the individuals that have been holding my hand from the beginning.

Mama, my soul mate, my savior, my best friend. I cannot begin to express my gratitude for your strength and action in saving my life. You have taught me everything I know about loving others as well as myself, about how to confront what is uncomfortable and grow from it, and how to see the light in every moment of darkness. You are the epitome of saving yourself. Mama, you are my inspiration and the only lap I ever want my crying little face in. Your tenacity and fierceness have demonstrated to me true power. I love you for endless lifetimes and am the utmost grateful that we get to share this one together, side by side.

My twin flame and brother, Cam, for all of the car drives you took with me to try to understand. For all the love you showed me when I couldn't show myself. For your adventurous spirit that will forever inspire me, I am so grateful. We've always had a bond like none other but you played a part in building me back up when I had lost myself. I love you isn't a sufficient enough statement.

Angela, my amazing therapist, I cannot thank you enough for the coping skills toolbox you've built with me, the validation you've provided, the insight into healthy relationships with others and myself, and all of the laughs and tears we've shared. I can imagine all of the ways my recovery could have gone wrong without you and I am eternally grateful that *you* were the one that came into my life when I needed you the most. Cheers to all of our future work together!

To my dad, I think we have taught each other some of the most valuable lessons about acceptance and mutual respect. Our ups and downs have led me to become the person I am proud of today and allowed me to realize our beautiful newfound connection. Thank you for allowing me space when it was necessary for me but being a foundation that I can fall on without exception. You hold such a special place in my heart.

To Wendy, my high school guidance counselor, that was the first person I attempted to explain my relationship with food to. You were such an essential backbone in my journey with your open heart, understanding, and undying love. I can always say you pushed me in the direction of loving myself and challenged my perfectionism and self-harming coping mechanisms. And a big thank you to your arms for always holding me while I was crying or shaking. My smile today is in many ways thanks to you. My gratitude towards you will perpetually be overflowing.

To my best friend Lucia, for always trying to understand my struggles and support me in the most tender ways. I know you came into my life as the person you were always meant to be; you have lifted me up when I was down countless times and made me belly laugh when I thought there could never be any laughter again. Saying I love you is not big enough.

And to all my incredible friends and family that I could list until the end of time, you know who you are, and you know my pure love for you. A gigantic thank you to my entire support system for ensuring that whenever I fall, I will be caught.

Oh and my dear readers, I could never forget about you! Thank you for picking up this book and squashing all the stigmas about eating disorders while doing so. YOU are forever worthy.

Bryn's therapist, Angela, Bryn and KC at the NAMI
Seeds of Hope scholarship awards ceremony.

Bryn's High school graduation with KC

Bryn's Kindergarten graduation with mom

The final quote

*"Just when the caterpillar thought the world
was over, it became a butterfly"*
~Anonymous

Resources

Maudsley Source for Parent Support:
http://maudsleyparents.org

NEDA- National Eating Disorders Association (Feeding Hope): https://www.nationaleatingdisorders.org/
1-800-931-2237

ANAD- Anorexia Nervosa and Associated Disorders (Eating disorder Hope)
https://anad.org/
1-855-783-2519
anadhelp@anad.org

Eating disorder help, hope, info:
https://www.eatingdisorderhope.com/information/anorexia

NAMI- National Alliance of Mental Illness
https://nami.org info@nami.org
1-800-950-NAMI (6264)

NIMH- National Institute of Mental Health
https://www.nimh.nih.gov/index.shtml nimhinfo@nih.gov
1-866-615-6464

National Suicide Prevention Lifeline
https://suicidepreventionlifeline.org/
1-800-273-8255

Children's Hospital Colorado
https://www.childrenscolorado.org/mentalhealth
720-777-6200

Colorado Crisis Services
https://coloradocrisisservices.org/
1-844-493-TALK (8255)
For more clinical information:
https://eatingdisordersreview.com/

Printed in the United States
by Baker & Taylor Publisher Services